179

Shallow Waters

HOUGHTON MIFFLIN COMPANY   1981

Shallow Waters

A Year on Cape Cod's Pleasant Bay

William Sargent

Photographs, pages ii and 137, *Cape Cod Times* Photos by Milton Moore

Map, page vi, by John V. Morris

Library of Congress Cataloging in Publication Data

Sargent, William, date
    Shallow waters.

    Bibliography: p.
    1. Marine biology — Massachusetts — Pleasant Bay.
2. Pleasant Bay (Mass.)   I. Title.   II. Title: Cape
Cod's Pleasant Bay.
    QH105.M4S27   574.9744′92   81-2581
    ISBN 0-395-29481-9   AACR2

Printed in the United States of America

P 10 9 8 7 6 5 4 3 2 1

To my son Benjamin,
in hope that he will also love the bay

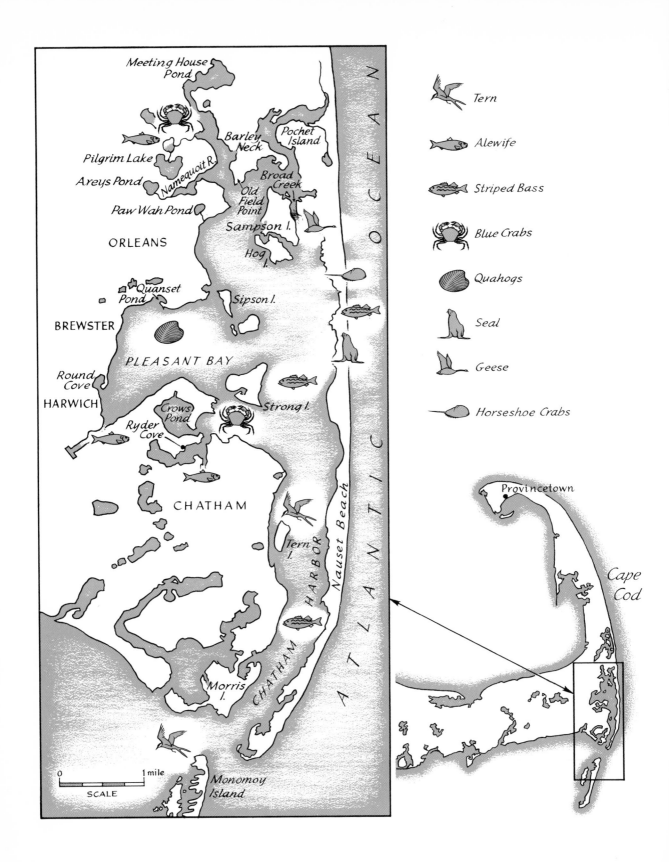

Meeting House
Pond

Barley
Neck

Pochet
Island

Pilgrim Lake

Namequoit R.

Broad
Creek

Areys Pond

Old
Field
Point

Paw Wah Pond

Sampson I.

ORLEANS

Hog
I.

Quanset
Pond

Sipson I.

BREWSTER

PLEASANT BAY

Round
Cove

Strong I.

HARWICH

Crows
Pond

Ryder
Cove

CHATHAM

Tern
I.

Nauset Beach

CHATHAM HARBOR

Morris
I.

ATLANTIC OCEAN

0   1 mile
SCALE

Monomoy
Island

Tern

Alewife

Striped Bass

Blue Crabs

Quahogs

Seal

Geese

Horseshoe Crabs

Provincetown

Cape
Cod

Contents

Illustrations

Herring gulls (Ralph S. MacKenzie)

BLACK-AND-WHITE PHOTOGRAPHS

Foreword

To Ken Read

Ken Read was my mentor in our mutual quest to understand the life of Cape Cod's Pleasant Bay. We spent ten years walking its shores and marshes, diving in its creeks, and photographing the behavior of its most minute creatures.

I met Ken for the first time at Harvard University's Museum of Comparative Zoology. My roommate had invited me to one of Harvard's sacrosanct rituals, the daily brown bag lunch at the museum's Department of Mallacology.

We entered the museum through a basement side door. Immediately we were surrounded by huge plaster casts of dinosaur tracks and assailed by the heady smell of formaldehyde. To this day, that smell stirs my imagination and remains intimately linked with the remembrance of an intellectual awakening.

The stern visage of Louis Agassiz stared down at us. Did he deem us qualified to undertake the painstaking task of gathering knowledge to pass on to future generations? I doubted it. I humbly followed my friend down an aisle between a hippopotamus and two lion cubs, preserved forever in their glass cases. We mounted the stairs near a gorilla beating his breast, passed under the suspended skeleton of a sperm whale, and rang the bell to the mallacology department.

We were then led down the long dark corridor of shelves to the inner sanctum itself. I felt like Alice being presented to the Mad Hatter's Tea Party. Seated around the table, brown bag lunches spread out before them, were people who shared the same odd passions that I felt. They had studied nature and traveled the world; they could answer my questions and understand my demons.

I had stumbled fortuitously into the very midst of the intellectual life that I had been seeking. However, no one took particular notice of my excitement; the group was locked in one of its famous discussions. Loud, boisterous, witty, opinionated; the arguments swung wildly from the role of deodorants in the ruination of America's sex life, to politics, and to collecting snails in pre-Castro Cuba.

Ken, sitting at the head of the table, was in command, pressing on, questioning, adding insights and relating stories of underwater discoveries in exotic corners of the world. Someone made a point: Ken lifted his head. His deep Welsh baritone boomed out over the already high decibel level: "Good God, you know you are right!" followed by his infectious staccato laugh.

Ken had discovered another truth. Truth was a passion with him; he loved truths better than anything. He liked them big or small. The best were the truths he discovered about human folly. He took a special interest and pleasure in unearthing a truth about his own inconsistencies.

From that first encounter we developed a relationship that was to shape my life forever. For twelve years I knew him better than I knew anyone else. We shared experiences diving in his beloved Salt Pond in Maine and filming mating sharks in the Florida keys. But most significantly, we investigated, explored, and speculated on Pleasant Bay.

Some of the best times I remember with Ken were during our long drives back from Cape Cod. Somehow we would pack all our photographic and diving gear into his dilapidated Volkswagen. On those trips Ken would delve into his latest discovery, a new book or theory.

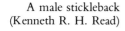

A male stickleback
(Kenneth R. H. Read)

Ken Read with a blue crab
(William Sargent)

Ken was a born teacher, a consummate, all-consuming teacher. I remember one evening in particular: We had just returned from the Cape and stopped for a bite in Schraffts, a small restaurant in Boston. It was late. There were only a few other customers sitting on stools around us. Our conversation in the car had carried over to the restaurant.

Ken was explaining why deforestation was so devastating to tropical soils. He was becoming increasingly animated on the subject, snatching handfuls of napkins to illustrate nutrient flow through a tropical jungle. The waitress, fascinated by the sketches, began to ask him questions. Soon a woman in her eighties joined our conversation. She was followed by the man seated at her right.

For at least forty-five minutes all activity in the restaurant ceased. Half a dozen people caught for free the intellectual fervor for which Ken's Boston University students had to pay tuition.

In 1977 Ken died in his laboratory. To the end, his life had been a search for truth. The search had been a good one. He pursued it with passion, knowledge, and love. Everyone who came near him was drawn into that search; some he taught how to think, others how to see, a few lucky ones he taught how to live.

I often think of Ken at the end of a long day of diving in the bay. As I lug the heavy equipment home, I pass a shallow creek. Ken and I spent the better part of three summers lying in six inches of water photographing the tiny creatures that reside there. I can see him now, rearing up out of the water, pushing back the mask that always made him look slightly comical, and exclaiming:

"That was fantastic! Did you see that leech parasitizing the shrimp? I have never seen that before."

Many times while preparing this book I have made a similar discovery, been perplexed with a question, or arrived at a tentative conclusion. It is then that I miss Ken most keenly. I want to be able to sit at the kitchen table with him and discuss the day's observations.

I have tried to record my observations faithfully and accurately. In places I have tried to apply new interpretations to some of the dynamics of evolution in the bay. My hope is that I have done my job well enough so that Ken, if he were to read it, would look up and exclaim, "Good God, Bill, you know you might be right!" Then I would know that I have succeeded.

Many people have been unceasingly supportive in helping me to study the bay and write this book. I am deeply indebted to the South Branch Foundation and the MIT office of Sea Grant, who provided initial funding to support a film series about the oceans. Nikon lent me the camera equipment that made these photographs possible. The Association for the Preservation of Cape Cod supported a weekly radio show about the bay. *The Cape Codder* printed my column about the bay and allowed me to use some of their black-and-white photographs in this book. Earthwatch Expeditions sponsored research on the bay. Esther Johnson and George Buckley shared many moments of enthusiasm and discovery on the bay. The New England Aquarium lent me photographs from the Kenneth R. H. Read collection.

John Teal of the Woods Hole Oceanographic Institute, Ian Nesbitt of Audubon, and Mick Rhodes of NOVA read my manuscript and made valuable comments. Daphne Abeel and Harry Foster, my editors at Houghton Mifflin, gave me help in preparing the book. I would like to thank Barbara Morrill for proofreading the manuscript and Lois Randall for copy editing it. Copenhaver Cumpston designed it.

Finally, I would like to thank my parents and my wife, Claudia, for putting up with innumerable students, friends, and scientists who flowed through our house using equipment and consuming untold quantities of food and fuel.

Each high tide deposits a ring of eelgrass along the shore. (William Sargent)

A pair of geese feed on the Spartina grass. (William Sargent)

Spring

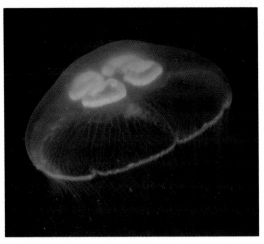

Medusa of the moon jellyfish
(Kenneth R. H. Read)

Spawning alewives (Kenneth R. H. Read)

Lonnie's River (William Sargent)

Spartina alterniflora (William Sargent)

A male stickleback guards his nest.
(Kenneth R. H. Read)

Creeks and ponds of the springtime marsh (William Sargent)

Summer

The bay at sunset (William Sargent)

△ The bay at full tide (William Sargent)   ▽ A squid (Kenneth R. H. Read)

▽ Silversides swim beside a redbeard sponge. (Kenneth R. H. Read)

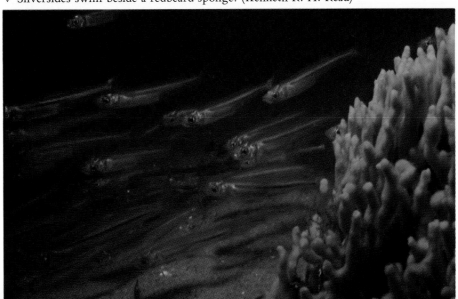

Autumn

A hunting boat floats in the autumn creek. (William Sargent)

Sunrise on the marsh (William Sargent)

△ A common eel   ▽ A blue crab (Kenneth R. H. Read)

▽ A ctenophore (L. P. Madin)

▽ The blue-eyed scallop (Kenneth R. H. Read)

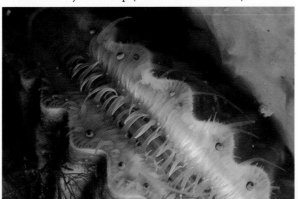

Winter

Pleasant Bay (Peace River Films)

Nauset Beach (Peace River Films)

Introduction

On the East Coast of North America the flexed arm of New England juts far out into the open Atlantic Ocean. This is Cape Cod, famous for its beaches, its history, its seafaring way of life.

Encompassed within the elbow of this fragile peninsula lie the shallow waters of Pleasant Bay. They ripple behind the low sand dunes of Nauset Beach and lap the sculpted bluffs of the western shore. This bay has been my summer home for my entire life.

A small wooden bridge spans a tidal creek. This bridge was my first laboratory. From its slight elevation I started to observe the habits of animals riding the flooding and ebbing tides: Some came to eat, others to mate, and others to lay their eggs.

I threw small scraps of fish into the creek to see which animals emerged to consume the feast. Gradually I learned which minnow would be first to snatch the bait and which crab would dominate the underwater battles for the best morsels. I noticed that some animals possessed minor differences in behavior, which gave them a slight edge in living and reproducing in the bay.

My horizons expanded from the creek, to the channels, to the oceans beyond. Masks and snorkels gave me different perspectives into this new world. An insatiable urge to understand the world of water developed in me. The urge became a quest and the quest an absorbing career. My observation platforms changed from the simple bridge of my youth to those of oceanographic ships, Russian trawlers, offshore oilwells, and a seat at the United Nations Law of the Seas Conference.

Research led me to the coasts of Africa and South America. It sent me to dive with whales in the North Atlantic and with

My son sits on the bridge where I first studied the bay. (William Sargent)

mating palola worms in the tropics. Most rewarding of all, the quest led me to fascinating people — fishermen and scientists, divers and cinematographers, people who had gone down to the sea to return with a new understanding of a world so different from our own.

Yet, I never lost the urge to understand the bay. I wanted to return with new tools and new knowledge to try again. In 1973 the Center for Field Research funded a study of the bay. Gifted students were recruited from across the nation to aid in the research. During that first year they were housed in my attic. A spare room served as our laboratory.

We christened our operation the Cape Cod Marine Science Center. In summer the Center would surge ahead with admirable resolve. In winter it would languish precariously close to financial collapse. But we all gained new understanding of the bay.

In 1977 I received a call from John Borden and Neil Goodwin of Peace River Films. They were making a film about a pond and asked if I would help. I had to admit that I knew nothing about fresh water. However, I lent them some equipment and suggested that they consider making a film about the bay. They did, and in 1979 we started to chronicle a year in the life of Pleasant Bay for the NOVA science series film, *The Sea Behind the Dunes*.

The year on Pleasant Bay allowed me to return to my earlier preoccupation, observing the behavior of individual animals. In the interim I had acquired new insights by observing wild monkeys in the field. Now, instead of simply cataloguing behavior, I started to ask questions: Why did some animals reproduce sexually? What were the advantages of sex? Why did most male animals compete to mate with as many females as possible? Why did some other animals reverse these traditional roles? What was the purpose of death?

During my year on Pleasant Bay the significance of some of these behaviors began to emerge. There were sound evolutionary reasons for the way males and females behaved. There were reasons for sibling rivalry and reasons for competition between offspring and parents. There were evolutionary reasons for aggression, competition, and ultimately even for death.

Life, death, and reproduction are all parts of an ongoing process whereby living matter is recycled and evolved to create ever-newer forms. Without this process life itself would perish, unable to survive the changes of the universe.

Pleasant Bay is a microcosm of that universe. Every year the bay changes; the barrier beach grows, an inlet forms, silt accumulates. Somewhere among the billions of organisms created there are unique individuals imperceptibly more fit to survive in the bay's changing environment. Molded through antiquity from the unity of all living matter, they carry on the greatest of all experiments, that of life itself. This then will be the theme of our story of a year on the shallow waters of Pleasant Bay.

Spring has its first grip on the land. (Ralph S. MacKenzie)

Spring

As the season changes, spring seems to come while the tide is out and winter to creep back with the cold water of high tide.

JOHN AND MILDRED TEAL, *Life and Death of the Salt Marsh*

Pleasant Bay (Richard Kelsey)

1. A Spring Visit to Nauset Beach

Springs walks upon the dunes, but the ocean lingers on the edge of winter. Day after day the sun pours an increasing splendor on the ocean plain, a hard, bright splendor of light, but the Atlantic mirror drinks no warmth.

HENRY BESTON, *The Outermost House*

Nauset Beach awaits the sunrise. A faint rose hue is already advancing across the eastern sky. It is March 21, the first day of spring. I have taken the boat across the bay to welcome its arrival.

I had to navigate in darkness through the chain of glacial islands that run like vertebrae down the spine of the bay. The silhouette of their contoured forms stood out against the graying light of dawn.

The winds have shifted for spring. Now they blow gently out of the southeast, carrying the smell of the spring ocean. It is the tangy odor of teeming acres of phytoplankton. Offshore meadows of these microscopic floating plants are starting to turn the ocean green; soon they will supply food for spring's abundance.

The faint light of the rising sun strikes the surf as it skids toward Nauset, the twelve-mile barrier beach that protects the bay behind. This narrow spit of sand is the fragile barrier that makes the bay possible.

The beach, recovering from the ravages of winter, is different today from what it was yesterday and from the day before. Every tide creates a new beach, an altered reflection of the previous storm.

Winter's storms have clawed away tons of sand, which now lie in reserve as part of the offshore sandbars. Each long regular spring wave returns precious grains to the beach and deposits them in delicate tracings along the shore. Together these tiny rims of sand constitute the wrack line. It is a treasure chest of oceanic flotsam and jetsam, which marks the farthest incursion of the last high tide.

Pleasant Bay at dawn (William Sargent)

Gradually the waves are rebuilding berms, broad plateaus of sand that are the foundation for the wide beaches of summer. The process is so effective that beaches have been known to grow as much as two hundred feet in a single tidal cycle.

The sand has been transported from the glacial cliffs of Truro, twenty miles to the north. Unprotected by wide summer beaches, they were exposed to the full fury of winter gales. Huge waves tore great gashes from cliffs, sometimes eroding their sandy flanks as much as twenty feet in a single storm.

The sand is transported from Truro by longshore currents. The currents travel parallel to the beach in the runnels, the underwater ravines that run between the shore and sandbars. Along the outer arm of Cape Cod, the longshore currents flow south, propelled by the energy of the prevailing waves.

It is this constant destruction and renewal that makes Pleasant Bay possible. As long as the ocean rises at its present rate of a few centimeters per century and as long as the supply of sand remains, the waves and currents will continue their yearly repair of the barrier beach.

Farther up the beach there is evidence of what will happen

4

when the supply dwindles. Winter has left a section of the beach narrow, dangerously susceptible to a storm that could burst through to the bay beyond.

During the February blizzard of 1978 the fragile barrier was breached in seventeen places. Cold green Atlantic waters overwashed the dunes and swept into Pleasant Bay, leaving great tongues of sand in their wake. Dune vegetation was buried and clamflats smothered. Inlets formed but were quickly closed by longshore currents.

This is all part of a cycle that is rapidly transforming the bay into a marsh. During the past two hundred years the barrier beach has grown more than three miles to the south. When it becomes too narrow, storms break through and inlets are formed. The inlets allow huge alluvial fans of sand to spread into the bay. More sand is blown in from the overwash areas where dune vegetation once anchored it in place.

The bay becomes shallower and new territories are claimed by marsh grass. The bay is diminished, but the marsh grows. In the process the shallower bay becomes more biologically productive, a boater's nemesis but a naturalist's delight.

Pleasant Bay has always been a transitory feature dependent on vast geological processes that build, sculpt, and destroy the land. It was forged in the wake of the world's most recent ice

The beach is recovering from the ravages of winter. (*Cape Cod Times* Photo by Milton Moore)

The blizzard of '78 swept many houses out to sea. (*The Cape Codder*)

Erratic boulders left by the glaciers (William Sargent)

age. The mile-thick Laurentian glacier had advanced out of Labrador 40,000 years ago. It had scraped over mountains, exposed rocky outcrops, and carved the valleys of northern New England.

As the glacier advanced it acted like a giant rasp, tearing away boulders and plucking up sand, gravel, and clay. These materials became part of the icy matrix slowly creeping toward the region now known as Cape Cod. Here it stopped.

The glacier had encountered the warm coastal climate generated by the ancient Gulf Stream. Fog enshrouded the area as the two countervailing forces battled. As rapidly as the glacier advanced, the warming climate melted its leading edge. Along the coast, huge blocks of ice tumbled off the face of the glacier to become floating icebergs.

The glacier had been advancing by expansion. The weight of snow and ice pushing down on its center had caused the glacier to bulge out along its perimeter. It had thrust forward massive lobes of ice causing it to move, amoebalike, across the landscape.

Ten thousand years ago two of these glacial lobes lay, one on each side of Pleasant Bay. The Cape Cod Bay lobe curved westward toward the mainland, while the South Channel lobe stretched south and east over what is now the Atlantic Ocean.

As the Cape Cod Bay lobe melted it dropped its load of boulders, rocks, and gravel. This morainal till now forms the sculpted bluffs and headlands of the bay's western shore.

When storms breach the fragile barrier beach, tongues of sand spread into the bay. (Richard Kelsey)

The South Channel lobe deposited most of its morainal material on the floor of what is now called the Atlantic Ocean. Then the ocean was 240 feet lower. Much of the world's supply of water was still locked up in the mammoth glacier fields.

Some of the deposited material formed an island on Georges Bank, now an underwater fishing ground 180 miles offshore. As it was deposited it formed a narrow strip of land along the edge of the melting glacier. Paleo-Indians gathered there to hunt mastodons, wolves, and ancestral horses. Today, even the most venturesome fishing fleets stay clear of treacherous areas of Georges Bank where white water surges over shallow glacial ledges.

On land, the only visible remains of the South Channel lobe are a few erratic boulders that can trace their ancestry to northern New England. That, and the string of islands — Pochet, Sampson's, and Hog — that run down the spine of Pleasant Bay, adding character to its early morning silhouette.

2. Spring Arrives on Pleasant Bay

Spring is a time for the renewal of life. In a sudden reawakening incredible in its swiftness, the simplest plants of the sea begin to multiply.

RACHEL CARSON, *The Sea Around Us*

Spring has its first tenuous hold on the land today. The April sun has thawed the ground but winter lingers in the bay. Daffodils and crocuses have already bloomed, and tiny green leaves will soon emerge from the thorny stems of wild roses. I have waited for such a day to make my first dive of the year. It will require a thick wetsuit and full diving gear.

I load the underwater cameras, gas tanks, and outboard into an ancient wooden wheelbarrow. Formerly a pair of oars or a few sails were all the wheelbarrow had to carry to the bay. Now it struggles under the weight of outboard motors that seem to increase their horsepower with every passing year. A modern wheelbarrow would undoubtedly be more efficient, but it is somehow reassuring to use one that I remember from the time when I was too small to reach its handles.

The marsh is showing the first faint signs of spring's reawakening. A subtle fringe of green now lines the creeks and shore. Tender young shoots of cordgrass are piercing through the dull brown stubble of last year's growth. Gradually the verdant hue will overflow the creeks to flood the salt hay meadows of the upper marsh. A red fox (*Vulpes fulva*) is patrolling the wrack line. He freezes, ears pricked, tail erect. He pounces, then digs out a struggling mouse.

His mate is busily feeding her kits in a den burrowed in the bluff beside the marsh. Two years ago the same pair built their den in a dry culvert under our driveway. It was unusually easy to observe their behavior from my parked car. Every morning they sat in the sun on a tussock of grass in front of the den. The kits quarreled over the remains of mice, birds, and occasional rabbits dragged in by their hard-working mother. They played

8

The runt of the fox litter
(Jack Swedburg)

king of the mountain on a sandy slope. Biting and snarling, they practiced in play the behaviors they would later need to survive. As spring wore on, I observed the toll taken on the mother. She became emaciated and burdened with bloated gray ticks while her kits became fat and well groomed.

The smallest kit was my favorite. She made up in aggressiveness for her diminutive size. She was the runt of the litter and probably would have perished in a lean year. As food became scarce her siblings and mother would have seen that she ate last. She would have starved while her littermates stayed well nourished. Chance favored her that particular season.

I surprise a pair of four-foot-long black snakes (*Coluber constrictor*) mating on the beach and oblivious to my presence. In spring they are under the influence of their mating hormones and are far less timid than normal.

They are lying in loose, random coils with the lower portion of their bodies braided around each other. It is difficult to determine where one snakes ends and the other begins.

The warm sun shines down on their glistening black skins,

9

starkly silhouetting them against the pure white sand. Sensuous undulations ripple down the length of their spines. One stares at me with cold black eyes but seems too preoccupied with his own pleasure to interrupt the tryst.

I stand in a voyeuristic trance, mesmerized by the spectacle. Gradually the undulations cease and the couple untwine. They stretch out on the sand and rest for a few more minutes; perhaps to savor the experience, perhaps to soak up the remaining sun. Slowly they glide, one after the other, through the beach grass, slither up the bluff, and disappear into an invisible hole.

I load the boat and the annual spring tug of war with the recalcitrant motor ensues. Unlike the sturdy wheelbarrow, the motor is only a few years old, but planned obsolescence will soon require its retirement.

A cough, a sputter, a belch of blue smoke, and the battle is finally won. The motor catches and holds a moderately steady rhythm. I ease the boat around the sandbar and head down the bay toward Crooked Channel.

The bay is strangely devoid of life. There are no boats and few birds. The great flocks of winter ducks have forsaken the bay, and the summer birds have yet to arrive. The season pauses briefly on the surface while winter lingers in the waters below.

I suit up and slip quietly into the channel. Frigid water seeps into my wetsuit and envelops my body. Soon it will be heated by my body temperature, enveloping me in a warm aquatic cocoon.

Beneath the water's surface, the bay has blossomed with life. Swirling clouds of diatoms and dinoflagellates reduce my vision to a few inches. Diving is unrewarding, photography impossible. Dense clouds of microscopic phytoplankton have turned whole areas of the bay blue-green with their abundance. They are plankton blooms, underwater harbingers of spring that indicate that a dramatic chain of events is beginning to unfold.

During the winter the decay of plants and animals accumulated nutrients on the bay floor. As the spring sun gradually roused the bay from its winter torpor it heated the icy surface waters, which plunged to the bottom where they stirred up great clouds of nutrients. The nutrients now serve as fertilizer for the rapidly multiplying phytoplankton. Their dominion in the bay is to be short-lived, however; the reason lies along the bottom of the channel.

Here the waters are less turbid. A flickering miasma of minute animals hangs like a hazy cloud above the bottom. These are zooplankton, drifting animals that have just started to hatch, and they are already grazing on the microscopic plants of the phy-

Marks left on the beach by mating
black snakes (William Sargent)

toplankton. Soon their numbers will be increased by the larval
offspring of fish, shellfish, and crustacea. They will drift with
the tide for about a fortnight before settling to the bay floor to
take up their adult existence.

The spring overturn of nutrients has transformed the bay into
a vast nursery. Each day another species hatches to feed on
organisms that reached their peak of abundance a few days
before. It is a well-orchestrated drama, finely tuned to the rising
temperature of the bay. By late spring there may be as many as
3000 different species of planktonic larvae out of the millions of
individual animals in a single quart of bay water. Suddenly it
dawns on me that I am diving in the midst of a cosmic experiment. These teeming swarms of animals are the result of over
two billion years of evolution. Their ancestors originally lived
in other environments; either freshwater, marine, or terrestrial.
Now they live in a bay that is only ten thousand years old. Its
modern estuarine environment is one of the richest on earth, far
more productive than those from which they came. These animals are still in the process of evolving organs and behaviors to
harvest the bay's riches and reproduce in her waters. I can use
Pleasant Bay as my personal laboratory to study one of the great
unifying concepts of human thought, the theory of evolution.

Einstein's theory of relativity, Freud's theory of the unconscious, and Darwin's theory of evolution stand as three pillars
that support twentieth-century thought. Like its fellow concepts,
evolution is still being reshaped in the light of new discoveries.
We are beginning to understand the role of DNA and genes in
organic and behavioral evolution.

Before returning to the bay it is best that we introduce some
of the current thinking about evolution. Recent exploration of
our solar system shows that we are inhabitants of a singular
planet. We call it planet earth, but in reality it is the planet ocean,
for our life-sustaining ocean is one of the truly unique features
in the solar system.

Life appeared on earth by one of two methods. Either it
evolved from a fortuitous mixture of chemicals and circum-
stances on earth or it came into being somewhere else and arrived
on earth when all the conditions were right for its development.
Either way, it is awe inspiring to think that that tiny spark of
life, whether it came from space or evolved on earth, held the
potential for the development of birds, bats, dinosaurs, and
human civilization. All that was needed was for evolution to
unfold that potential.

Throughout geological time the earth has been bombarded by
cosmic rays emanating from celestial bodies billions of miles

away. These rays alter the genes of living animals. Genes are crucial because they are the receptacles of the genetic code that determines what kind of cells will be produced.

Most of these mutated genes are deleterious. They cause cells to produce defective organs or they cause an animal to behave strangely. In essence, most of these mutations are mistakes. However, some mutations cause an animal to have a slightly more beneficial organ or to act in a way that makes it better able to cope with the environment. The most significant aspect of evolution is that it is a system for preserving these valuable mistakes.

The vehicles for incorporating these mistakes and passing them on to future generations are the genes. But there is a kicker. The easiest mistake to make about evolution is to assume that evolution works for the sake of the species or for a population or even for the sake of an individual animal. It does not. Evolution works on the genetic level. It works primarily for the perpetuation of a line of genes.

Chemical differences between the make-up of genes and the rest of an animal's cellular material has led some scientists to speculate that originally there were two different types of living matter. The type that now forms our genes became totally dependent on living within the cells of the other type of animal. The bacteria-like "gene animal" could not live without inhabiting host animals. The host animals could not replicate without their alien genes. In essence then, animals are parasitized by their own genes.

Some scientists have even speculated that animals can be thought of as hardware and their genes can be thought of as software. The animals are like disposable robots only necessary for housing genes. As in computers, the software is the critical element. The genes are in control of the robots and make them behave in ways that are advantageous to the genes, not to the robots.

Perhaps we can look at two examples to see how this might work. If genes are partially responsible for behavior then we can see how behavior could evolve. When a mother puts herself in jeopardy to protect her offspring it is not advantageous for her but it is good for her offspring. Thus it could be argued that it is advantageous to the species or the genes.

But how can we explain runtism? It is common among animals so it must have some survival value. It is clearly not advantageous to the individual, if in most instances the individual dies. It is difficult to make the argument that it is good for the species. The species would not be helped if runtism became the

The sun has warmed the bay from its winter torpor.
(Ralph S. MacKenzie)

13

A larval starfish
(Woods Hole
Oceanographic Institute)

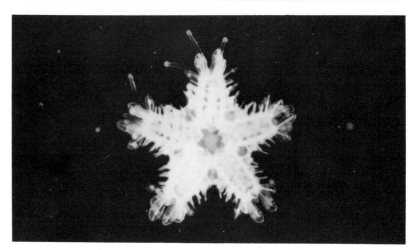

The same starfish one week later
(Woods Hole
Oceanographic Institute)

norm. If genes are responsible for runtism, then it is possible to make an argument for its persistence.

If a pair of foxes could raise five kits during a normal year, then during a plentiful year they might be able to raise five kits plus a runt. They would have raised six kits while foxes without the genes for runtism could raise only five. They would have increased their chances of passing on their genes by one fifth.

If evolution works this way, then perhaps we can understand why animals sometimes act against their own best interests. It is always tempting to assume they behave altruistically for the benefit of the species, but in reality it may be for the benefit of their selfish genes. We will return to the significance of these selfish genes when we see how different animals have evolved behavioral repertoires to exploit the riches of Pleasant Bay.

14

3. A Day at the Herring Run

I watched the fish at the top of the ladder as they jumped over the broad dam to meet at last the quiet stretch of pond water above it. The waters were growing green with algae as the seasons developed, and were penetrated by deep shadows, blue shafts from the sun, yellow and pink reflections from the spring leaves on the bank.

JOHN HAY, *The Run*

This morning I decide to visit one of the many herring runs that feed into the bay. This run is a small brook that flows into Lonnie's River. The river's gentle curves are already trimmed with the sharp green shoots of emerging cordgrass.

I slow the boat as it rounds a bend. The surface of the river is dimpling with reflected sunlight. Each time the bell-shaped body of a jellyfish breaks the surface, the sun glints off its shining mass.

The river is choked with the opalescent pink bodies of the moon jellyfish (*Aurelia aurelia*). They have timed their appearance to take full advantage of the spring plankton blooms.

Near the edge of the river there is another type of jellyfish. A rarity in the bay, the Lion's Mane jellyfish (*Cyanea capillata*) is already larger and redder than the two-inch moon jellies. By the end of the summer, it will be eight feet across and it will trail a hundred-foot tangle of deadly tentacles.

Its tentacles have now captured two moon jellies. The three are locked in a deadly ballet, each dancing to the silent rhythms of its own water-filled body. The unconscious synchrony has carried them into the sharp underwater blades of grass. Soon the dance will be over. Each pulse will draw a stem deeply into a fragile body. The tortured medusae will weaken and die, their brief tenure as sexual beings will be over.

These jellyfish recapitulate one of the most significant steps in evolution, that giant step from asexual to fully sexual reproduction. During the winter, the parents of these free-swimming jellyfish were stationary pink polyps that lined the peat along the

15

The herring brook (William Sargent)

sides of the river. They looked like inconspicuous flowers that snared plankton as it swept by with the tide. Only two weeks ago, the bay's rising temperature triggered a profound change within their quarter-inch bodies. They grew and segmented. Each segment became a rhythmically pulsating animal. Finally, one by one, the tiny medusae tore away from the stalked bodies to drift off with the tide. This is an asexual form of reproduction called strobilization.

Perhaps the rapidly changing environment of the bay provides a clue to the intriguing question of why animals evolved sex in the first place. If the ancestors of these jellyfish lived in a more stable environment, like the ocean, asexual reproduction would suffice. In fact asexual reproduction would be preferable because it would allow them to clone exact copies of themselves, copies that were already preadapted to the environment.

However, if they had been trapped in a rapidly changing environment like the bay, they would have been doomed. They, too, would have to change. One strategy to achieve this change was to "invent" sexual reproduction.

Sexual reproduction enables an animal to produce offspring with a new mix of genes. These genes could help it arrive at a new and unique solution to one of the problems of living. In essence, then, sex speeds up evolution.

In the case of the jellyfish the ability to survive the seasonal rigors of the bay has enabled them to exploit the bay's vast quantities of plankton. Their asexual ancestors were destined to remain in the less productive waters of the ocean.

Close to the edge of Lonnie's River, a lone herring (*Alosa pseudoharengus*) looms out of the depths and swims unerringly toward the herring run, a small brook with a concrete fish ladder that descends from a pond above. The herring, more properly called an alewife, stops and swims about hesitantly. He has encountered a disturbing interface, the turbulent area, where the fresh waters of the brook mix with the salt waters of his marine home. He tastes the water. Can he detect the faint chemical traces that indicate that this is his parent stream, the one he tumbled down as a fingerling nearly four years ago? His acute senses are giving him information on salinity, oxygen, and acidity.

The alewife is joined by two more. They mill about cautiously, their senses warning them that this is a strange, potentially dangerous environment. However, the changing season has triggered their hormones, and their imperative cannot be denied. Their bellies are full of the next year's generation, and they have found their parent stream. With a final rush, the tiny

16

Lonnie's River (William Sargent)

school leaps over the first step of the fish ladder. They will have to battle the swollen spring torrents all the way to the quiet waters above. Many will die, but those that reach the pond will remain there for a few weeks to lay and fertilize their eggs.

Some of the herring have already accomplished their mission. One of them is slowly descending the fish ladder. He faces into the current, gasping to remove what little oxygen the fresh water can hold. There is a large white patch on his back. He has been pecked by a sea gull. The mishap has removed the coating of slime that protects him from infection. A freshwater fungus now infests the spot.

His odyssey has been harsh, but it will soon be over. The salt waters of the bay will kill the fungus and he will start to feed again. His body will readjust to the increased salinity, and he will survive.

Beside him is another fish that will probably not be so for-

A sea gull attacking alewives (*Cape Cod Times* Photo by Milton Moore)

tunate. It is a freshwater sucker (*Catastomus commersoni*), which has been swept out of the pond. Now he hugs the gravelly bottom of the brook between attempts to swim back upstream. He is, however, a poor swimmer, unfit to battle against the rushing water. Each attempt only sweeps him farther downstream. Inexorably, he descends to a certain death in the salty waters below.

Similar incidents must have occurred frequently during the early development of the bay. This area was a series of small upland ponds connected by a river that ran south through a cold, bleak glacial environment. Runoff water from the melting glaciers must also have swollen the annual spring floods. Undoubtedly, many freshwater fish were swept out of the ponds and into the newly forming bay. In its rich estuarine waters they discovered limitless supplies of plankton and small fish.

Those fish able to survive the gradual change in salinity were abundantly rewarded. Their eggs, however, could still not survive in salt water. Gradually, fish evolved that could migrate back to fresh water to spawn. The obstacles to such evolution were great, but the advantages were legion. Their offspring, no longer dependent on the limited supply of food offered by the pond, could afford to lay many more eggs. The eggs and larval fish were protected in the pond during their first summer of growth. After they had passed through those most vulnerable

18

stages they were able to descend the herring run and exploit the abundance of the ocean. It is easy to see that the fish that evolved this behavior had a far greater chance of producing more offspring than those that did not. They developed what animal behaviorists call a stable evolutionary strategy, one uniquely adapted to exploiting both the protection of the pond and the abundance of the ocean.

But it is time to surface and head toward home, where a small wood-burning stove will restore movement to my frozen fingers. High overhead, a flock of eider ducks are migrating toward the Arctic tundra. These spring migrations are far less evident than those of autumn. Few birds stop to rest on the bay. Mostly they fly unseen during the night.

Birds migrate more rapidly in spring because it is crucial to the success of their breeding season. They will fly to their breed-

Migrating eider ducks (*Cape Cod Times* Photo by Milton Moore)

The heart of the weir becomes a thrashing maelstrom of fish. (*Cape Cod Times* Photo by Milton Moore)

ing grounds where they must select mates, build nests, and raise their families during the short Arctic summer. The males arrive first and stake out nesting territories. Those birds that leave late will be more successful at passing on the genes that trigger a later migration.

But now the sun is setting, and the air is a cool reminder that it is time to return. Skimming homeward in the fading light, I hurtle toward a flock of fifty brant. They have lingered on their eelgrass feeding grounds before departing for the Arctic to breed. They burst from the water and fly to a sand bar at the mouth of the creek. In the old days, a market hunter might have been waiting for them. Spring shooting was the custom then, but this evening the birds merely mark the end of a warm spring day when life floods the bay with its abundance.

4. Night Fishing on Nauset

It is as if the writhing rivers of moving fish, pulsing through the Atlantic's submerged arteries, also set the fishermen's blood to coursing with the same elemental energy . . . That is the magic that rides on the striper's shoulders as it swims through the ageless pattern of its annual migration along the shore and deep into the souls of the men who live on it.

JOHN COLE, *Striper*

Every day more boats are appearing on the bay. A few hardy souls have been going out since April to fish for flounder, but it is not rewarding. The winter flounder (*Pseudopleuronectes americanus*) spawned in March. Now they are thin and spent. Fishermen refer to them as "windowpanes" because they lack the firm tasty flesh of autumn. As the bay warms they will migrate to the cool deep waters of the Atlantic. They will be replaced by summer flounder, "fluke," that have spent the winter offshore.

May 5 is the date the bass usually return to the bay. As the date approaches, fishermen keep a close watch on each other. Each boat carries a casting rod and a full selection of plugs. When no one is watching we all take a few "pokes" in some of our secret spots.

Cape Codders become unusually taciturn when asked about the incoming bass. Writing about the bay gives me a cover of sorts. A few days ago a friend pulled up beside my boat and confided, "Them Powell brothers caught two schoolies in their weir yesterday. Mebbe we'll be ass deep in 'em by Memorial Day."

Schoolies are the immature striped bass (*Marone saxatilis*) that still travel in schools. They hover either side of 16 inches, the legal taking size for bass in Massachusetts.

The weirs are large fish traps, remnants of what was once a thriving business up and down the East Coast. During their heyday such fish traps yielded 25 percent of the fresh fish sold on the Northeast seaboard. These deep-water traps are driven in as soon as the ice flows out of the bay. They are little changed from those built by coastal Indians hundreds of years before the arrival of European explorers.

The trap consists of a leader, a heart, and a bowl. The leader, a 900-foot vertical net that stretches toward the shore, interrupts the great underwater migrations of spring and autumn. When the migrating fish encounter the leader they instinctively head out to sea toward the waiting heart of the weir.

Trap fishermen empty the weirs every morning. They pull their boats into the heart and purse the bowl, raising the bottom of the net toward the surface. The bowl becomes a thrashing maelstrom of fish. They are bailed into trap boats with large dip nets called "kill devils."

In March the Powells started catching herring; alewives, blue-backs, and bunkers. Later they will catch squid, scup, bonito, and bluefish. It is all part of a vast collection of animals migrating toward the rich feeding grounds off Pleasant Bay. To the waiting fishermen all these fish are of little importance. They await the arrival of the bass.

The bass are migrating from their breeding grounds in the tributaries of Chesapeake Bay. The immature schoolies lead the migration, followed by the adults. Large "bulls" migrate last. The "bulls," actually misnamed, because they are females, can be as old as 40 years and weigh up to 100 pounds.

When the bass finally do arrive, people flock to the bay with all manner of fishing gear. Many fishermen go directly to the herring runs to scoop out alewives which they will use as live bait. Others use eels or troll elaborate umbrella rigs that look like whole schools of bait fish. It is generally thought that the bass follow the herring into the bay just as the terns follow the silversides up the coast. It is more likely that each species of fish, crab, and bird is responding to its own biological clock.

The biological clocks of birds are set to respond to the increasing length of daylight. This is because temperatures fluctuate so rapidly on land. Underwater the reverse is true. In spring the temperature of the water rises gradually and steadily, triggering the hormones that control the migratory and mating behavior of fish.

One of the best ways to grasp the dynamics of the underwater migration is to go night fishing on Nauset Beach. Many people drive beach buggies down the long narrow spit, but I prefer to take the boat across the bay. It is best to arrive at the beach before sunset and return on the nighttime high tide.

It is still low tide when I arrive at the "back shore." The boat runs aground fifty feet from the beach, so I have to anchor it

Parallel tracks along the shore (William Sargent)

there. When I return at high tide I will have to wade through
the shallows carrying gunny sacks heavy with striped bass.

The sun is sinking and the bay is calming. The wind has
shifted from onshore to offshore. By day the warmer land draws
a cool breeze off the ocean; by night, the warmer ocean draws
a cool breeze off the land. Thick sweaters and clumsy waders
will protect me from the nighttime chill.

A few fishermen have already arrived on the outer beach. One
is digging for sandworms to use for tonight's bait.

I search in vain for migrating whales. Humpbacks, finbacks,

23

and minkies hug this shore on their annual spring migration from the Caribbean breeding grounds. They feed on schools of bait fish in the rips and runnels just off the outer bar. As a boy I remember seeing them feeding just off the beach.

The water was brown with schools of the tightly packed menhaden. "Pogy" boats from Long Island had followed them north. They were running seines around the compact schools squeezed in the gullies between the bars. Suddenly one of the schools exploded into a fusilade of silver projectiles. Frantic, footlong bodies leaped clear of the water. The sun caught the silver spectacle for a moment before the huge open mouth of a whale erupted from the spot. Hundreds of fish spilled from his mouth, while thousands more were engulfed in one swallow.

The whale's heavy dark body burst free of the surface. It hung, eerily suspended in the sunlight, before plunging back into the cobalt blue waters. A cascade of water rose in its place. Huge tails slapped the surface. Whales were scaring the menhaden into revealing their position. Their acute hearing would pick up the vibrations of the frightened fish as they rushed toward the surface. Perhaps I read too much purpose into their actions. They could be signaling each other or merely expressing excitement, celebrating the joyful feast.

Their feeding was a vivid example of the accelerated flow of

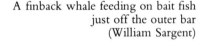

A finback whale feeding on bait fish
just off the outer bar
(William Sargent)

nutrients up through a food chain. The night before, part of the menhaden had been molecules of inorganic matter lying on the ocean floor. That morning they had been converted to living vegetation by tiny motes of phytoplankton. By afternoon they had been consumed and tranformed into menhaden muscle. The next night would find them metabolically converted into whale blubber. Certainly this was a food chain rapid and simple enough to grasp: inorganic matter, to primary producer, to consumer, to predator in three easy steps.

A stranded skate (Peace River Films)

The sun sets and the tide turns. Currents course down the runnels between sandbars. Fishermen don their waders and gingerly step into the surf. They cast their tin jigs over the runnels trying to land them on the exposed sandbar on the far side. They flick the jigs into the water and slowly reel them home. The incoming tide does the rest. Strong longshore currents sweep the jigs south. They glint and flutter, creating vibrations that the bass will receive along the sensitive lateral lines of their bodies. The ability to sense vibrations in the water allows bass to be nocturnal feeders. It even allows them to survive when blind; inconvenienced though not incapacitated, they swim beside their sighted brethren.

The fishermen are standing in a teeming corridor of life. The narrow tunnel between shore and bar is a living river of migrating creatures. Silversides and herring struggle against the rushing current, while skates and rays seem to fly just above the ocean floor.

The moonlight catches the dark form of a bass silhouetted in the translucent curl of an incoming breaker. Crazed bait fish slam into my fishermen's legs, followed by the frightening hiss of a large bass as it slashes after minnows only inches from my waders.

We are starting to catch bass in the waist-deep water. It looks like the beginning of a blitz. Blows are almost exchanged as "meat fishermen," intent on catching fish for the market, crowd out a small group of recreational fishermen.

Competition is even more deadly below the surface. These bass started their life's odyssey in April two years ago. They were conceived in the brackish waters of tributaries of Chesapeake Bay. Their conception was on a scale almost beyond the scope of human comprehension. Amid opalescent swirls of milt and roe, male and female bass roiled the surface. Each large female was attended by two or three smaller males. They mated in a sensuous orgy of fecundity. Each female produced 600,000

pearly white eggs. After three days only 600 eggs remained. After six weeks only three inch-long fry had beaten the odds of survival. They were joined by thousands of fellow survivors migrating north, never more than three miles from the shore, never more than three miles from the pollution and hordes of fishermen that inhabit the largest industrial megalopolis of the world. Perhaps two would make it to the shallow waters of Pleasant Bay.

Striped bass have provided food to East Coast dwellers since the first paleo-Indians settled after the retreat of the glaciers. In 1614 Captain John Smith described schools of striped bass so thick that "it seemed that one mighte go over their backes drishod." Taxes raised from the sale of striped-bass fishing rights paid for the first public school built by the Plymouth colony.

The annual monetary value of the present East Coast bass fishery is estimated to be several hundred million dollars. It probably approaches the billion dollar mark if one takes into consideration the money spent by recreational fishermen on boats, tackle, food, and fuel. However, all this may soon change. Since 1970 the striped bass population has been declining rapidly. Overfishing is not the problem; pollution is. Ninety-nine percent of the East Coast population of bass spawn in the Hudson River or Chesapeake Bay. Of these, 90 percent that range beyond Long Island come from the Chesapeake. Both spawning grounds lie in the watersheds of one of the world's most overused land areas. Rivers of industrial chemicals and fertilizers flow off the land and into the breeding areas of the bass. These toxic chemicals are severely affecting the spawning vitality of the fish. Millions of eggs remain sterile.

Power plants destroy still more larval bass when they suck billions of gallons of water into their cooling units. John Cole, who researched the steady decline of bass for his excellent book, *Striper,* said in 1977: "Ten years from now, at its current rate of decline, the striped bass will no longer roam the inshore waters of the Atlantic . . . After that, I am not sure I shall want to live."

In 1980, I called him to get an updated opinion. He said, "It certainly doesn't look good, but I find myself hoping that somewhere out there in the mystery of a sea the striper is working to survive us all."

If striped bass disappear from the East Coast an irony will remain. The only large population of them will be on the West Coast. It will be composed of the hardy descendants of 107 bass that survived a transcontinental train trip to be introduced to San Francisco Bay in 1879. Today they proliferate from San Diego to Vancouver. Such fish are built for survival. The tough-

The catch
(Copyright © Gordon S. Smith)

A few ducks still dabble along the shore. (*Cape Cod Times* Photo by Milton Moore)

ness that allowed them to transplant so well is the same toughness that will allow them to survive in their East Coast spawning grounds if we prevent these from becoming nothing more than chemical dumps.

5. The Stickleback Pond

The shore with its difficult and changing conditions has been a testing ground in which the precise and perfect adaptation to environment is an indispensable condition of survival.

RACHEL CARSON, *The Edge of the Sea*

The buoys are in for Memorial Day weekend. Tender pink blossoms of *Rosa rugosa* tint the bluffs, and the sweet smell of honeysuckle fills the air. Thick deposits of pollen dust every surface and spread a yellow film along the shore. The pollen is from vast stands of pitch pines that are ancestors of the first reforestation program in America. In 1821, Chatham, threatened by drifting dunes, planted beach grass and pitch pines to save the town.

Long wet windrows of eelgrass glisten in the sun. Torn from the bottom of the bay in a late May storm, they are precursors of the vast mats of dying eelgrass that will cover the beach in summer and fall. A few ducks still dabble along the shore and egrets stalk fish in the shallows.

The marsh behind Strong Island is in its full spring glory. The creeks and shore are trimmed with dark green cordgrass. The upper marsh is cloaked in a soft verdant hue. The meadows have taken on the color of the tender shoots of salt hay.

This marsh probably came into being only 4000 years ago. By that time Egypt had already undertaken the construction of the pyramids, and Babylon was consolidating under Hammurabai. The sea level was still eighteen to twenty feet lower than its present level. That is the depth of most of the deep holes and channels in the modern bay. Salt water was starting to flood the two freshwater rivers that flowed down either side of the bay. The rivers built up a broad, shallow sand flat on the south side of Strong Island. The first marsh grass seeds probably arrived from the south on the feet of a migrating shorebird. Darwin once reported finding the seeds of seventeen species of plants caught in the mud on a duck's webbed foot.

The first Spartina seeds to arrive on Strong Island were nurtured by two crucial features on the island. The water was shallow, and freshwater runoff flowed down the steep bank. *Spartina alterniflora* seeds sprout in two weeks when bathed in fresh water, but take over two months to sprout in undiluted salt water.

When the *Spartina alterniflora* first colonizes a shallow water area it sends out rhizomes, underground root systems that start new plants. The complex root system catches mud and detritus to form a foundation of peat. The build-up of peat allows marshes to keep pace with the gradual rise of the sea level. Thus a marsh that is eighteen feet thick has been present for four thousand years — from the time when the sea level was eighteen feet lower.

As the peat builds up it prevents the high tides from flooding the upper marsh. The *Spartina alterniflora* is replaced by its cousin, *Spartina patens*, and a new environment is created, the dense meadows of fine salt hay. Early Cape Codders used the broad stretches of this grass to harvest hay for their cattle. They outfitted horses with special large wooden shoes to prevent their sinking in the soft wet peat. The hay was cured and piled on large wooden straddles on the high marsh. At one time, Pleasant Bay's islands supported large herds of cows and sheep that grazed on their rich salt hay meadows.

The marsh became laced with creeks and dotted with small ponds. The ponds are formed when the Spartina grass creates a dam or when a patch of grass is killed. A mat of eelgrass lying on the Spartina could start the process. Without light the Spartina grass quickly dies. Its roots and rhizomes start to rot and a small depression appears on the marsh. The depression holds water, which hastens the process. Spartina grasses cannot survive in standing water. Like tooth decay, the mixture of trapped water and rotting vegetation eats a cavity into the peat. In young marshes the holes might reach all the way through the peat to the underlying sand. The ponds fill with Ruppia weed, a succulent water plant that is the favorite food of wigeon ducks.

This confusing maze of creeks, Ruppia ponds, and Spartina grass thwarts me. The creeks are too deep to wade and the ponds too numerous to avoid. I am trapped in the heart of the marsh. As I attempt to find a way out I find myself comparing the ubiquitous ponds. Each pond contains a slightly different population of fish. Those ponds connected to the bay by creeks are awash with mummichogs. The ponds that are separated from the bay contain killifish and sheepshead minnows transformed by the mating season into brightly colored gladiators. Under the

RIGHT *Spartina alterniflora* fringes the creeks (Ralph S. MacKenzie)

30

Spartina patens cloaks the upper marsh. (Ralph S. MacKenzie)

influence of the rising water temperature these fish have sought out the ponds, during last month's spring tides. They will remain protected until the high spring tides return one month later.

One pond catches my attention. It is filled with striking red fish, which do not scatter at my approach. When I walk by the pond all of the fish rise to the surface and stare intently at me. All thoughts of crossing the marsh disappear at the discovery of this mystery. I will enjoy the day unraveling the curious behavior of these fish. I sit down to see what will happen. Nothing happens. All the fish scrutinize me with strikingly blue eyes. The fish are obviously agitated and will not settle down.

I cannot imagine why they are upset. Suddenly I realize it is my appearance. It is still chilly so I am wearing a red-and-black plaid lumber jacket. To the fish I look like a huge male stickleback, on the make and ready to defend my territory. I take off the offending jacket and lie on it. Within minutes the fish quiet down. I experiment by flashing the red lining of my camera case toward the pond, and the fish become agitated again.

These rubicund little fish are male sticklebacks (*Gasterosteus aculeatus*) in full courtship colors. The Nobel prize-winning animal behaviorist Konrad Lorenz once had a similar experience with sticklebacks. He used to keep an aquarium of them in his office. He noticed that every day at 8:15 all the male sticklebacks would become very agitated and swim to one side of the tank. He could not find the cause of this behavior until one morning he happened to be looking across the street and noticed a large red Austrian postal truck picking up the 8:15 mail. The sticklebacks were crowding to the side of the tank, responding to the truck as they would to a rival male.

I start to see things I had not noticed before. Each male is about ten inches from his neighbor. They are all in red courtship colors and are busily defending their aquatic territories.

The males are guarding nests in various stages of construction. Some have only started digging pits in the sand, while others have already completed their nests. They have hauled pieces of Ruppia weed into the sand pits and have fashioned them into leafy arches that fit snugly around their bodies.

The ten-foot pond is too crowded for the territorial sticklebacks. One male is down in his sand pit completing his tunnel. A neighboring stickleback approaches the invisible barrier that separates their territories. The first fish rushes out of his pit with color flaring, fins erect, and gill covers spread. He looks like an outraged landowner, face flushed and ready to drive this trespasser off his property.

The first fish assumes a vertical, head-down, threat position. The intruder approaches more closely. The owner dashes toward him, then retreats to the vertical position. He starts to butt the sandy bottom as if he were starting another nest. He is caught between the dual drives of wanting to fight and wanting to flee. He resolves his ambivalence by displacing his aggressions in this violent mock nest-building activity. His solution can be compared to kicking a door when one is really angry with one's boss — kicking the boss could have severe economic consequences.

The intruding fish approaches the center of the owner's territory. The violation is too flagrant. The owner rushes out and beats the water rapidly with his tail. The shock waves travel through the water and slam against the sensitive lateral line that runs the length of his rival's flank. It is a forceful way of expressing his machismo. Undaunted, the intruder does the same. They are sizing each other up, testing each other's strength.

A male stickleback courts a gravid female. (Kenneth R. H. Read)

33

Suddenly the owner pommels the flank of the intruder with his snout and tail. The intruder retreats, with color faded and fins retracted. The owner gives chase. As he approaches the edge of his territory, however, his aggression diminishes. He returns to his nest building. The invisible boundary between their territories has not changed.

Elsewhere in the pond I notice a female. She lacks the red color of the males, displaying instead the distended abdomen of her gravid or pregnant state. She is having a difficult time in the crowded pond. Like a lone girl in a singles bar, she finds her way constantly blocked by ardent males. She swims quickly through most territories, but one male draws her attention. She swims into his territory and pauses. He rushes at her as he would an invading male, but she does not respond to his threats. She hangs passively, subtly turning her swollen abdomen toward him. It is this female response that triggers his next move. He swims seductively toward his nest and pauses to fan the tunnel with his tail. This is the same motion he will use to aerate the eggs. Is it a ritualized movement to show that he will make a good father? She seems reluctantly curious. He approaches again, repeating the enticing zigzag dance. She follows and stops. He is courting her ever closer to their conjugal bed.

Finally she follows him to the nest. Like a gentleman, he stops and indicates the entrance by moving his head. She precedes him into the tunnel, where she lays her eggs under the influence of his vigorous caresses to the base of her tail. Each ritualized move has to be followed by the correct answering gesture for the courtship to succeed. The courtship is almost over. She wiggles out of the tunnel, and he follows her into the chamber to fertilize the eggs. While he is occupied with this, the final act of the courtship, she swims away, never to see her eggs or offspring again. He will remain to protect and aerate the eggs until they hatch in early summer.

What can we make of the elaborate courtship of the stickleback, which seems so removed from the casual relationships of the bass and herring?

Sticklebacks have discrete signals, sign stimuli that mean but one thing. In the male it is the red courtship color; in the female it is the distended abdomen. Each sign stimulates a specific response in the other fish. The same is true with other animals. A male robin will attack an inanimate red feather duster that resembles the red breast of a rival male, but he will ignore a living competitor whose feathers have been dyed another color.

A male stickleback will gamely court all manner of inept female facsimiles as long as they have a ventral hump that is vaguely reminiscent of the swollen abdomen of the gravid female. These signals are particularly well developed in fish. Fishermen have inadvertently exploited them to advantage in selecting fishing tackle. Experienced fishermen know that the best fishing lure is not the one that is the most naturalistic copy of a bait fish but the one that most outrageously exaggerates a particular signal; a flash of silver, a streak of red, or an erratic swimming movement.

In the herring we have seen the continuation of reproductive behavior not much different from that of the "discoverers" of sex, the invertebrates. Like the moon jellies, the female herring lay vast quantities of eggs. The males fertilize them externally, and the eggs are left to the vagaries of the environment. It is the quantity of offspring released rather than the quality of nurture that makes this profligacy successful.

The sticklebacks represent an advanced form of nurture that we generally associate with higher animals. The female produces relatively few eggs, which are carefully protected and nurtured. In the herring, males and females are virtually indistinguishable, and courtship is brief and simple. In the sticklebacks, there is a striking difference between male and female, as well as an elaborate courtship display. If we look at the physical environment

An alewife (Ralph S. MacKenzie)

of the bay we might find an answer to the success of both evolutionary strategies.

Herring return to the relatively stable environment of the freshwater pond to achieve their random spawning. Sticklebacks, however, spawn amid the adverse changing conditions of their intertidal spawning pools. They must combat the fluctuations of temperature, oxygen, and salinity that occur with each high tide. They are not allowed the luxury of leaving their eggs to nature's whim.

It is easy to see how the environment necessitates the evolution of nurturing parents to protect offspring. It is more complex to understand how evolution determines which parent will do the bulk of the parenting.

Herring simply let the eggs fend for themselves. Other animals (like eagles) are monogamous and share the nurturing equally. Many animals, however, require the nurturing efforts of only one parent.

Single-parent nurturing leads to an evolutionary version of the war between the sexes. We have already seen that evolution works by passing on genes to future generations. A parent that mates and then leaves has the potential for breeding with several other mates while its original partner raises the family. The abdicating parent thus has a greater chance of passing on more genes.

In most species it is usually the female who does the bulk of the parenting chores. Pregnancy makes it impossible for her to leave her offspring after mating. If the necessity of pregnancy is removed, females are as likely as males to abdicate their parental responsibilities.

A female stickleback without the burden of internal fertilization is free to leave her eggs with the male. She can whisk off to mate with several other males while he remains to raise her offspring.

Fish as a class have experimented with so many different types of reproductive behavior they are becoming favorite subjects for animal behaviorists. As more scientists go underwater they will find other examples of the evolution of behavior. We, too, are products of evolution; therefore, their findings will also help to unravel some of the mysteries of human behavior.

Sticklebacks, in fact, have become the white rats of animal behaviorists. Anyone can keep an aquarium full of sticklebacks beside his desk and watch their fascinating courtship displays. Of course it is far more satisfying to discover their behavior in a small marsh pond on a warming spring day.

RIGHT A snowy egret leaves the marsh. (William Sargent)

36

A small alluvial fan spreads into the bay. (William Sargent)

Summer

Cool breath of eastern ocean, the aroma of beach vegetation in the sun, the hot pungent exhalation of fine sand — these mingled are the summer savour of the beach.

HENRY BESTON, *The Outermost House*

6. A Swim Across the Bay

I begin to reflect on life's eagerness to sow life everywhere, to fill the planet with it, to crowd with it the earth, the air and the seas.

HENRY BESTON, *The Outermost House*

Spring has slipped imperceptibly into summer. Profligacy has waned into a steady abundance. The creatures of the bay will use this abundance to grow, to feed their offspring, and to store protein against the winter's scarcity.

Occasional catspaws ruffle the mirrorlike surface of the bay, and the sun wraps the world in a hazy cloak of warmth. The incoming tide is spreading across the sandflats, which are yellowish green with a thin slime of diatoms that thrive on the nutrients flushed off the marsh with each high tide.

As I walk across the sandflats, they emit a shivaree of subtle sounds. Their inhabitants are preparing to gorge themselves during the brief high tide. A pair of toadfish (*Opsanus Tau*), glower at me from beneath a boulder. They have dug a shallow pool beside the rock where they will brood their young. The female lies upside down beside her mate. She is assiduously affixing their large orange eggs to the roof of the watery grotto.

I wade out into the incoming tide. Pink blobs of translucent jelly sway and bob in the shallow waters. These are the egg cases of the lugworm (*Arenicola marina*). Like earthworms, they feed by ingesting large quantities of sand to consume the diatoms that cover each grain. The clean sand is then deposited in neat little cones on the flats. In a year they will clean over a ton of sand on this half-acre area.

The water is warm. It has been heated as it flowed across the sunbaked sand. I follow a translucent school of silversides as they skitter across the sun-dappled bottom toward the deeper waters of the eelgrass beds.

Eelgrass (*Zostera marina*), the pervasive weed that fouls people's tongues as it fouls their outboards, is the mainstay of the bay. Unlike other seaweeds, Zostera was originally a flowering

The sun wraps the world in a hazy cloak of warmth. (Ralph S. MacKenzie)

41

A toadfish (Kenneth R. H. Read)

Oxygen bubbles rise from
photosynthesizing seaweed.
(Kenneth R. H. Read)

A puffer fish (Kenneth R. H. Read)

land plant that evolved to live in estuarine waters. Its thick blades anchor silt to the mudflats and release oxygen into the water, making the phenomenal productivity of the bay possible.

In 1931 an epidemic disease attacked the eelgrass. It spread up and down the East Coast until thousands of acres of eelgrass withered and died. The loss of oxygen and nutrient-rich detritus at the bottom of the food chain set off a devastating domino effect. The fish and shellfish populations crashed, followed by those of the ducks, geese, brant, and shore birds. Some researchers blamed the disease on a fungus, others on Labyrinthula, a curious parasitic protozoan that feeds on the weakened plants. A total environmental disaster was averted when a strain of Zostera, somehow immune to the disease, accidentally appeared in Pleasant Bay. State and federal officials have since replanted most of the East Coast with descendants of Pleasant Bay eelgrass.

There is a relative paucity of visible animals in the Zostera beds. The bottom, now five feet below me, is all but obliterated by the thick fronds of eelgrass. Each blade is bejewelled with bubbles of oxygen. As I separate the fronds, silvery cascades of bubbles stream through my fingers, travel up my arms, and burst against my faceplate. I seem to be flying through a field of pearls. Tiny white coiled shells of Spirorbis worms festoon each blade, making them rough and scratchy. My body is being alternately scratched and caressed in a long sensuous massage.

Spirorbis borealis has evolved an elaborate pseudo-pregnancy. The worm mimics a mammalian pregnancy by holding its eggs in a brood chamber after they hatch. This protects the offspring while they develop into larvae. The red-eyed larvae are released into the bay on the quarter moon's neap tide, the weakest tide of the month, which will not sweep them away from the eelgrass beds. They swim for only an hour before settling on a new blade.

The well-timed system is so efficient that the worm only has to release twenty eggs at once. Other worms and mollusks must release millions of eggs, which have to survive a fortnight of massacre before settling to the bottom.

I stop to hover over a thick tangle of eelgrass fronds. A few spider crabs, clinging to great armfuls of eelgrass, peer up at my intrusion. They look like tree monkeys clambering through the top of a jungle canopy, shaking branches to threaten me, the predatory eagle flying over their domain.

By midday I reach Crooked Channel. Ken Read and I spent many days photographing fish in these clear waters. Heavily weighted, holding our cameras in one hand and the anchor of the boat in the other, we let the outgoing tide carry us downstream. When we spotted a sea robin with only its eyes showing above the sand, we would simply drop the anchor and glide to the bottom where our weight belts held us firmly to the substrate. The boat would wait patiently overhead like a well-trained horse who had just lost his rider.

Lured with quahog bait, the sea robins move in rapidly from downstream. We could see them sensing the water with the fingerlike rays of their pectoral fins. If we approached too close, they would use the outstretched fins to threaten us.

Sometimes we saw lady crabs (*Ovalipes ocellatus*) mating in the sand. Squid (*Loligo pealii*) would hang motionless before us, with waves of color racing down their bodies. Each flash of the underwater strobe would send them darting away. Then they would stop and allow us to approach again.

Stopping to rest on a sandspit that juts into the main channel, I stir up sediments to attract minnows out of the green depths. Now I am surrounded by a cloud of silversides and confronted by a friendly puffer fish (*Spaeroides maculatus*). As I reach out to scratch his belly, which will make him puff up and rise to the surface, I start to laugh at the ludicrous sight.

Suddenly, I have the distinct feeling that my foolish antics are being watched. I look up. Only inches from my faceplate is the snaggle-toothed grin of a shark. Granted, it is only a three-foot dogfish, but I beat a hasty retreat back to the shallow eelgrass beds.

A pipefish hangs vertically in the water; its long, thin body cleverly mimics a swaying frond of eelgrass. I start to pass by until I notice another larger, brighter pipefish suspended nearby.

I realize I have blundered upon a courtship ceremony. I am fortunate, for the pipefish's courtship is a rarity in the animal kingdom. The female approaches the male and displays her courtship colors with what can only be described as abandon. She nestles and caresses his body, swimming about with an ever-increasing pitch of excitement. The reluctant male is finally cajoled into presenting his abdomen. She, with what seems like gleeful audacity, inserts her genital papilla deep into his belly slit.

There she deposits several hundred eggs and swims off, leaving him alone and pregnant. He will now have to suffer through three weeks of pregnancy and the agonies of labor before ridding himself of the burden of single parenthood.

Pipefish are sexually dimorphic. Sexual dimorphism is a term that means that one sex of a species is larger than the other. In most animals the male is larger. Animal behaviorists have observed that sexual dimorphism usually goes hand in hand with

The incoming tide (William Sargent)

polygamy. Thus male seals form harems and male lions form prides of females. Homo sapiens are also slightly dimorphic. As expected, human males tend to be larger and are reputed to be slightly more promiscuous.

What of the female pipefish? She is larger and more sexually aggressive than the male. Does she refute this observation? Let's look at the evolutionary reasons for sexual dimorphism to find an answer.

We have determined that evolution occurs when genes are passed on to future generations. Males produce many more sperm than females produce eggs. Thus a male has many more chances of passing on his genes than a female. A female has a better chance of passing on her genes if she makes sure that her limited number of eggs and offspring reach adulthood. Thus males and females rely on different methods to achieve evolutionary success. Males tend to mate as often as possible while females tend to nurture their offspring. Animal behaviorists call these methods evolutionary strategies.

If a female can be evolutionarily successful by nurturing her

A goose shepherds her family along the edge of the marsh. (Ralph S. MacKenzie)

offspring it follows that she can be even more successful if she finds a male who will also provide some of the nurture.

In pipefish, evolution has gone one step further. The male provides not some of the nurture but all of it. The female is able to assume the usual male role of promiscuous breeding. At least among pipefish, women's liberation has achieved a resounding success.

Does this disprove the theory that males tend to compete among themselves to mate with females that will be effective mothers? No, it seems to support the theory in its more general form. The sex that assumes the bulk of the parenting is competed for by members of the opposite sex.

But I have reached the shallow flats near Hog Island. I surface to see a mother goose shepherding her family along the edge of the marsh. I wonder if she is aware of the great evolutionary significance of her role? The sun sets deeper and finally disappears behind the western shore. I have completed my swim across the bay.

7. At a Horseshoe Crab Orgy

Underlying the beauty of the spectacle there is meaning and signifi-
cance . . . it sends us back to the edge of the sea, where the drama of
life played its first scene on earth; where the forces of evolution are
at work today, as they have been since the appearance of what we
know as life; and where the spectacle of living creatures faced by the
cosmic realities of their world is crystal clear.

RACHEL CARSON, *The Edge of the Sea*

The moon is full. There is no wind. There are no sounds, save
for the gentle lapping of the water against the shore. It is the
ninth of July. The beach quietly awaits the flood tide, the highest
of the month. An expectant sense of creation fills the heavy night
air, for it was in warm shallow waters like these that life first
evolved.

Offshore, a female horseshoe crab prepares to re-enact a ritual
that has persisted for over 300 million years. Heavy with the
weight of hundreds of small green eggs, she advances slowly
toward the shore. She must crawl through a stag line of smaller
male horseshoe crabs that have been attracted by pheromones,
chemical aphrodisiacs, that she released into the still waters.
Males clamber to attach themselves to her shell. Often females
emerge from the water dragging two or even three eager suitors.
The dark forms of the crabs appear in the silvery luminescence
of the shoreline as they start their long crawl up the beach. The
quiet scraping and scratching of their shells can be heard as they
scramble over each other in their eagerness to lay and fertilize
their eggs, for soon the tide will turn, stranding them to the heat
of the morning sun.

The female starts to dig into the moist sand just below the
high tide mark. Her strong sand-pushing legs propel her deeper
until she almost disappears. After resting she starts to deposit
her eggs. Hundreds are released, then the males fertilize them.

By this time the beach may be covered with hundreds of crabs
laboring to lay and fertilize their eggs. As the tide recedes they
return to the life-sustaining waters of the bay.

The next day I brought Neil Goodwin and John Borden to the site to film the scene by daylight. We witnessed a drama that would be a compelling sequence in their NOVA production about Pleasant Bay. We set up a battery of underwater and surface cameras well before the arrival of the crabs. We were on the inside of Nauset Beach. A few years ago this spot had witnessed the fury of a winter storm as it burst through the sand dunes. The frigid waters of the Atlantic washed over the barrier beach and deposited a giant tongue of sand in the shallow waters at the edge of the bay. Gentle waves had sculpted the raw sand, and Spartina grass had anchored it in place. Now the terminus of the outwash was a sandy crescent that encompasses a shallow pool. The pool was to prove crucial to the drama that was about to unfold.

The incoming tide swept around the sandy horns of the narrow arc, and hundreds of crabs followed it. The shallow pool teemed with lustful horseshoe crabs. Dozens of males swarmed around every female, or anything that could possibly be mistaken for one. They surrounded the tripods of our cameras and explored our feet with lascivious abandon. It became so distracting that John and I had to haul them off of Neil's feet so that he could concentrate on filming.

Eventually the tide turned and the crabs' plight became evident. The arc of sand continued to hold water while the tide dropped. The standing water did not give them the appropriate signal to depart. They remained preoccupied with their mating, unaware that they were about to be trapped in the small pool. The remaining water started to drain out through the sandy bottom. Panic gripped the crabs. Three hundred frenzied crabs swept clockwise around the rapidly dwindling pool. Some tried to climb over the arc, but most seemed resigned to their fate.

We couldn't be certain what signals they needed to trigger their return to the bay. The females seemed to wait for the tide to turn before they dug into the sand. This would ensure that the eggs would remain buried until the highest tides of the next month.

After they laid their eggs the normal behavior would be to follow the outgoing tide to deeper water. Climbing onto the sand would be exactly the wrong response. It was only the presence of the sandy arc between the crabs and the water that made that "wrong" behavior the "right" thing to do. Sometimes nature hedges her evolutionary bets by creating a few oddballs that act improperly. In some rare instances their wrong behavior will make them do the right thing. Perhaps we can extrapolate further to say that the evolution of a brain able to discern when

A horseshoe crab moves toward the beach. (William Sargent)

Male horseshoe crabs swarm over a female. (William Sargent)

The compound eye of a horseshoe crab (William Sargent)

Filming horseshoe crabs (William Sargent)

to act properly and when to act improperly is the best insurance of all.

Horseshoe-crab senses and behaviors were evolved over 300 million years ago. Could the crabs now be thwarted by an unexpected anomaly of the beach? Of course not. One by one they dug into the sand where they would be safe from the desiccating sun until the next high tide liberated them.

Farther up the beach, two horseshoe crabs were trying to contend with a problem for which evolution had left them defenseless. A family had walked over to see what we were filming. Satisfied that we were just filming "some old crabs," the parents drifted back to their beach buggy, but their two sons lingered behind, unable to resist hurling an empty beer bottle at the defenseless crabs.

The shells smashed with a sickening crunch. Thick blue blood spewed from a jagged crack in the carapace of one of the crabs. Green eggs oozing through the blood revealed that it was a gravid female. She crawled up the beach and into the sand. The other injured crab was a smaller male. His shell was also rent and his eye dangled uselessly against his carapace. Heeding my reprimand, the boys retreated to their beach buggy.

Ugly defenseless animals seem to evoke an intense hatred in man. Perhaps I spoke up largely out of guilt for I, too, had been a killer of horseshoe crabs. That was the tradition on Cape Cod. All youngsters were taught to kill them with impunity. We even had a dog that followed our example. He would spend long hours wading in the shallows feeling for the crabs with his paws. When he found one he would dunk his head under water and grasp it by the tail. He would deposit the crab above the wrack line. When it started to crawl he would dig a hole in front of it and bury the unfortunate creature after it tumbled into its grave. The technique was passed from dog to dog through three generations.

These actions by children and dogs are sanctioned by society. Until recently most towns on the Cape still gave bounties for horseshoe crab tails, and the state shellfish regulations recommended that horseshoe crabs be left above the high tide mark. Shellfishermen harbor a deep resentment against the crabs because of the damage they are purported to do to commercial shellfish.

Horseshoe crabs eat by masticating food on the bristles of their walking legs. It is not particularly efficient. The crab has to be walking and the food has to be soft or brittle. Their prime food tends to be worms and delicate *Gemma gemma* clams that look like immature quahogs. The only time that horseshoe crabs can feed on commercial species is during the few days that the larval shellfish lie on the bottom before digging into the substrate. The rest of the time horseshoe crabs probably help the bay by turning over the mud like ancient Paleozoic plows.

Horseshoe crabs (*Limulus polyphemus*) are actually not crabs but belong to the same class as spiders (*Arachnida*). Their ancestors were believed to be spiderlike creatures that lived in fresh water and fed on insects. They crawled about in shallow waters long before there were dinosaurs and thus can truly be called living fossils.

They are remarkably adept creatures. They come equipped for nearly any eventuality — except dogs and children. Like spiders, they possess numerous eyes. In addition to the two obvious compound eyes, they have median eyes that detect ultraviolet light and several others that merely look down into the mud.

The General Electric Company has studied the eyes of horseshoe crabs in order to improve television reception and to develop lenses for concentrating solar energy. A Nobel Prize was awarded for some elegant research done on the receptor cell of the horseshoe-crab eye.

Horseshoe crabs are protected with a hard outer shell that prevents injury from almost every predator except man. They possess a tail that looks lethal but is actually used for righting themselves when they are caught on their backs. Several times during the year I saw a horseshoe crab that had lost his tail. Unable to right himself, he wallowed in the shallows, buffeted by the smallest wave. By the end of the summer he was dead.

Under their tails, horseshoe crabs have a set of book gills, large fleshy flaps that look like pages in a book and double as paddles when the crabs swim on their backs. These book gills are larger versions of those found on modern spiders and help establish their relatedness to the *Arachnida*.

It is the blood of horseshoe crabs, however, that makes them one of our most valuable marine animals, demanding prices once reserved for lobsters and oysters. A quart of processed horseshoe-crab blood is worth over $15,000. It may provide an answer for understanding and curing cancer and it has already saved hundreds of lives from spinal meningitis.

Horseshoe-crab blood is blue because it is copper-based, unlike our own red, iron-based blood. The blood retains an anti-infection system that is elegant in its primitive simplicity. When a horseshoe crab is wounded, large amoebocyte cells migrate to the affected area, and coagulate. The entire area is simply sealed off with a viscous plug so that no infection can infiltrate the wound. I have seen horseshoe crabs with large segments of their bodies missing. They simply isolate the area and continue their life, waiting for the next time they shed their shell to start regenerating the missing portion of their body.

Scientists have discovered that these blood cells can be made into a powerful new biological test. The horseshoe-crab blood is processed into Limulus lysate, which can detect minute amounts of endotoxins released by Gram-negative bacteria. Gram-negative bacteria are as deadly as they sound. They receive their name from a test that reads negative when they are present. Gram-negative bacteria are pervasive in our bodies. They live in our intestines, where they do little harm. However, during shock or illness, the endotoxins can permeate the membranes of the intestines and infiltrate the blood stream. The result can be fatal.

Spinal meningitis is one of the fatal diseases caused by Gram-negative bacteria. The disease often requires treatment within 48 hours to prevent damage to the central nervous system and even

A horseshoe crab isolates a wound with coagulated blood. (William Sargent)

death. Limulus lysate is an exquisitely sensitive aid in diagnosing the disease. It replaces the earlier rabbit fever test that required seven days to perform. The Limulus test is a thousand times more sensitive and can be performed in less than an hour, a crucial margin.

Researchers have also found that endotoxin impurities in drugs used to treat cancer patients often proved more beneficial than the drugs themselves. This has led to the experimental treatment of malignant cancer tumors with endotoxins. Limulus lysate's ability to detect subtoxic amounts of endotoxins may lead to the controlled therapy of cancer with this method.

In 1974 I became involved with a project trying to prevent the depletion of horseshoe crabs in Pleasant Bay. Limulus lysate had just been developed, and collectors were sent to the bay to gather crabs for the new drug. I was working with a group of students from the Cape Cod Marine Science Center. It soon became apparent to us that the collecting was seriously affecting the bay. The entire population of horseshoe crabs had dwindled, and it was difficult to find any of the large females preferred by the bleeders. We held a meeting to decide how to deal with the matter. Half of our crew wanted to sabotage the collecting boats while a small minority preferred to try to reason with the infidels.

The debate lasted late into the night. Finally, after gallons of cheap wine were consumed and effective arguments were made, the democratic process prevailed. We voted to negotiate with the bleeders and dispatched a small but persuasive delegation to Woods Hole. They returned with a deal. We agreed to collect the crabs as long as we could experiment with returning them to the bay.

In the open water of the bay we built large wire pens twenty feet long and six feet high. The day before the truck was due to arrive our crew could be found wading around in waist-deep water collecting horseshoes. Inevitably, by the time the truck arrived most of the crabs had found a hole in the chicken wire and escaped. Those remaining were loaded into the truck for shipment. A few days later they were returned to us. We carefully put them back into the pens and fed them crushed mussels.

After a few days they recovered from the bleeding. We meticulously marked each crab and released it. We experimented with several types of markers. The most whimsical proved to be balloons that we tied to the horseshoe crabs' tails. For a day the bay would be full of colorful animated balloons crisscrossing the quiet surface.

The results of our experiments proved rewarding. By pres-

53

Collecting horseshoe crabs (William Sargent)

suring the bleeders we were able to persuade them to extract only a safe amount of blood. The mortality was reduced to less than five crabs out of every hundred bled, thus proving this latest threat to their survival to be surmountable.

Limulus polyphemus continues to plod along the floor of Pleasant Bay like an aging bureaucrat. The successful evolution that has allowed him to live unchanged for 300 million years gives him strength in the simplicity of his systems. He can live for a year without eating and like the cockroach can survive radiation that would kill a human.

The human race, like its culture, has grown increasingly complex. The human body is defenseless against many of the diseases caused by mankind's own pollution. The horseshoe crab has seen the dinosaurs come and go. Perhaps somewhere in the recesses of their primitive brains the dinosaurs felt they ruled the world. Will we use our modern brains to so rule the world that we leave it once again heir to the horseshoe crab and the cockroach?

8. A Visit to the Tern Colony

Like silvery sailplanes, common terns ride spring winds high above the cold waters of Cape Cod. Courting pairs weave zigzag patterns as they glide down toward their nesting colony.

DR. IAN NESBITT, *National Geographic*

The bay is flat calm this morning. The early morning sun glints over the barrier beach, casting a pink sheen on the oily waters. A few patches of gossamer fog hang over the bay, reflected in its mirrorlike surface. The wake from my motor stretches out behind me rending the waters like a cruel white scar. Fortunately it is one of man's only temporary affronts to the early morning peacefulness.

Suddenly in the distance the calm is broken. A small flock of terns (*Sterna hirundo*) has gathered over a school of fish. The raucous cries of their feeding spread excitement around the bay. Other terns, attracted by the calls, start flocking in from all directions. By the time I reach the spot there is a frenzy of anticipation. Hundreds of these feisty, graceful birds jostle for position before plunging into the frothing green waters. Often they arise with the writhing body of a silversides minnow held crosswise in their bills. The water is churning with dismembered bodies, blood, oil, and terror. Swirls, boils, and an occasional leaping fish indicate that large bluefish are below. The silversides have been riding the incoming tide across the shallow flats. The currents have swept them over the lip of sand into the deep channels where the bluefish lunge out in ambush. The hapless silversides are caught in a terrifying crossfire. Huge bluefish hurtle out of the green depths below and swift terns dive out of the blue sky above. Massacre is everywhere. Schools of frightened silversides leap free of the water only to be driven under again by the two vanguards of voracious predators.

Occasionally a tern will leap into the air in fright as a bluefish makes a pass at its dangling feet. The terns are careful to dip

55

only their bills below the surface. When they feed over the slower bass, terns will plunge entirely into the water. Bluefish, however, will gladly tear off a tern's leg or rip into its plump white breast. In the midst of their feeding frenzy, the bluefish slash back and forth through the school of minnows, severing them without returning to eat the remains. Viscera from the massacre spread an oily slick across the water's surface. Twitching bodies of half-eaten silversides drift quietly down through the gloomy green water.

As suddenly as it started, the feeding frenzy is over. The bluefish sound and do not reappear. The terns fly off in search of other schools or return to their nesting sites, each holding a choice fat minnow crosswise in its bill. Thus laden, they fly unerringly to their nests on Monomoy Island. In fog, I have used their return flights to lead me back to land.

Monomoy is a continuation of the Nauset barrier beach that projects far south into the teeth of the Atlantic. From the air, Monomoy can be seen reaching across treacherous shoals toward Nantucket Island. When the rising ocean and longshore currents have completed their work they will have transformed Cape Cod into a long barrier beach that will finally reach Nantucket. The terns have nested on Monomoy extensively since 1962, when the Department of Fish and Wildlife removed the predatory foxes. This year there are about 6000 nesting terns on the island.

As I top the rim of grass above the beach, I am overcome by one of nature's great sights. Thousands of birds wheel and turn in the sky above me. The noise is deafening; the smell pungent. The terns, descending to hover over me like a swarm of angry wasps, start to dive at my unprotected head. Sharp raps from their bills can draw blood. I stoop to protect my face and to watch out for chicks and eggs. As the day wears on, I become shell-shocked, flinching uncontrollably in anticipation of the next attack. From time to time I feel a strong urge to run screaming to the tranquillity of the beach.

It is late in the season. The nests are in all stages of development. Most contain two eggs, some have chicks, some are empty. Hundreds of spotted chicks scurry around and hide in miniature copses of goldenrod. Scattered around the site is evidence of a bad year. Many eggs have not hatched. Chicks sprawl dead on the sand. An adult tern lies decapitated, dried blood oozing from its neck into the sand. A foot away an older chick hides trembling in the grass beside its younger sibling. The culprit is a great horned owl. Every night he has swept across the colony, killing adults and chicks. The adults have started to

A tern carries a sand eel back to the nest. (Ralph S. MacKenzie)

stay away from their nests, and the chicks are dying from the unseasonably cool weather.

The family of the decapitated parent shows the slim margin for error in tern reproduction. The mate of the dead tern continues to bring minnows, but the older chick monopolizes all the incoming food. I watch the younger chick grow weaker, trembling in the pitiful clump of grass, scant inches from its dead mother. The evening chill will kill this chick, but with luck the older one will survive.

The nesting area offers many lessons in how evolution works. Terns are specialized to capitalize on a rich source of food. They have to expend a great deal of energy diving for the live minnows. Adult terns have to fish continuously to feed themselves and supply the 25 to 30 minnows a day required by each chick. Some adults are better fishers than others and could raise three or four chicks. Since most adult pairs can safely raise two eggs, that is the average number laid. The eggs are laid two days apart

but hatch one day apart. If ocean conditions alter so that the bait fish do not appear, then the older chick will get what little food there is and survive. If both chicks were to split the food equally, both would probably perish. Natural selection has evolved a system of egg laying to minimize the risks of their reliance on a precarious food supply.

These terns also show how new behavior can evolve. A few terns lay more than the average two eggs. In a good year when food is plentiful these terns may be able to raise three chicks, thereby increasing by one third the probability that the genes for laying three eggs will be passed on. If the ocean conditions were to improve permanently then this behavior could spread through the population. Evolution would have selected terns that lay three eggs over those that lay two.

The terns are visited by a host of predators. Owls, hawks, foxes, even sea gulls and night herons eat the defenseless chicks. Ants enter the newly cracked shells and kill the chicks before they can fully hatch. The greatest threat to the terns comes from the herring gulls. Besides being gluttonous predators, they compete with the terns for nesting sites. Just down the beach from the terns is a raucous colony of nesting gulls.

If terns, with their specialized eating habits, are the gourmets of the shore, the sea gulls are the gluttonous gourmands. They will eat anything, particularly the garbage cast off from human gluttony.

There is an artificially large number of sea gulls on Cape Cod. Thousands of them can be seen sitting around any town dump. Without the dumps their numbers would be culled by the harsh winters. Their opportunistic eating habits allow them to exploit their proximity to man. Like rats, pigeons, and other scavengers they are so successful that they crowd out less opportunistic species like terns.

The wily terns have another ingenious device for increasing their evolutionary chances. I notice that most of the terns in an area lay their eggs at about the same time. The proximity of other breeding females seems to bring the nesting terns into reproductive synchrony. A classmate of mine discovered that the same thing holds true with human females. She used the girls in her Radcliffe dorm as guinea pigs. She found that most of the women in her dorm started to menstruate at nearly the same time after they had lived together for a while. Other studies indicate that sexual scents similar to the pheremones that released the reproductive drive in horseshoe crabs cause this behavior. It would seem to fulfill little functional purpose in a Radcliffe dorm. In a tern-nesting colony, however, one can discern the

The chicks hatch one day apart.
(Leslie A. Campbell)

59

slight advantage gained through safety in numbers. If the eggs were laid at random times, an owl would be able to kill the chicks one by one on each nightly raid. When all the chicks are raised at the same time it increases the chances that only a few will fall victim while the others prosper. The terns are protected through safety in numbers when they are in reproductive synchrony.

I make my way to a blind set up by Ian Nesbitt, an ornithologist who studies terns for the Massachusetts Audubon Society. Once I am in the blind the colony starts to settle down. Directly in front of me on a small patch of sand a female tern alights in a male tern's territory. She squats into the sand and he approaches her. He holds his head erect and allows his wings to drop. The female seems transfixed by the display. He starts to prance around her. Crouching in the sand before him, the female swivels about in the sand. By the end of this courtship display she has created a small depression that will eventually become their nest. All the adult terns are extremely territorial, even mercilessly attacking chicks that wander into the wrong territory. Close by, another male tern is presenting a minnow as a gift to his mate. Scientists feel that this gift is the sine qua non that stimulates the female into mating. Curiously, this female is a hybrid, the result of mating between a common and a roseate tern. This is very rare. It indicates that the two species have not yet evolved enough to be fully separated reproductively.

I leave the breeding birds and walk through the colony again. Normally, people should not walk through a breeding colony of terns. During the day an intruder will scare the parents off the chicks and they will die from the heat of the sun. However, it is an unseasonably cool, overcast day, and I have received permission from Dr. Nesbitt.

There is a slight ridge running through the nesting site. This area has been occupied by laughing gulls, beautiful white birds that sport jet black heads during their breeding phase. Their distinctive "ha ha" call is reflected in their name. This colony used to nest on Muskegat Island off Nantucket. Since 1972, when hurricane Agnes swept waves over the island destroying all the nests, the gulls have shared Monomoy with the terns.

Many species of terns nest on the island: Roseates and common terns share the elevated beach grass areas, while artic and least terns nest on the open sand and shingle. These subtle differences in nesting behavior tend to keep the species as separate reproductive groups. Farther down the beach the gulls provide another example of the way speciation works.

A male tern starts the courtship. (William Sargent)

The herring gulls are just finishing their nesting activities. Chicks, if a bird larger than a chicken can be called a chick, hide in high patches of beach grass. The adult gulls are just as protective as the terns. They sound like planes when they attack, but fortunately they only hit with their feet, not their bills. The herring gulls share a common ancestor with the lesser black-backed gull in Northeastern Siberia. The two populations started to move apart. After millions of years they met again, halfway around the world on the East Coast of the United States. The lesser black-backed gull had arrived from the east and the herring gull had arrived from the west across America. When they met on the East Coast they were two distinct species. Their body forms had changed slightly, but more important, their reproductive behavior had altered. The herring gulls had acquired a breeding season that started two weeks earlier than the breeding season of the lesser black-backed gull. The two groups of animals were thus effectively prevented from reproducing with each other. They had become separate species because of reproductive isolation. The inability of two groups of animals to reproduce when put together is what determines a species. Even dogs, which come in all shapes and sizes, are considered to be one species because they can all breed with each other, though a dachshund would have a tough time with a Saint Bernard.

61

A courting male tern presents a sand eel to a female. (William Sargent)

The marshy side of the island contains hundreds of shore birds. Their names often indicate the feeding behaviors they have adopted to exploit the rich intertidal area. A pair of ruddy turnstones busily root through the marsh like feathered pigs, turning over stones and shells in search for crustacea and worms. A small flock of oystercatchers poke about for blue mussels. They are able to work their stout bills into mollusk shells to snip the abductor muscles.

Suddenly there is a great disturbance on the marsh. A short-eared owl has been spotted by the tern colony. More than a hundred terns are already mobbing it. More are flocking in to peck and harry the cumbersome flyer. After each attack, little clumps of owl feathers drift out of the sky to land on the marsh. The flock's vigorous common defense seems to work. The owl lumbers along steadily toward the west, where a Wagnerian sunset silhouettes the aerial duel. It has been a long day. The colony has started to settle down.

Tonight after dark one tern will give an alarm call and the entire flock of 6000 adult terns will rise high into the sky where they can be seen flying against the full moon. None will be present to heed or hear the tiny peeping distress calls of the chicks as the dark shadow of the great horned owl sweeps down over the colony, silently taking his nightly toll.

9. A Midsummer Storm

The dune bank there was washing away and caving in under the onslaught of the seas, and presently there crumbled out the blackened skeleton of an ancient wreck which the dunes had buried long ago. As the tide rose this ghost floated and lifted itself free, and then washed south close along the dunes. There was something inconceivably spectral in the sight of this dead hulk thus stirring from its grave and yielding its bones again to the fury of the gale.

HENRY BESTON, *The Outermost House*

The morning has turned as sultry as midsummer in Venice — pregnant with anticipation of change. The heat creates mirages of the cabins that line the end of Nauset Beach. They seem to float in the heavy air at the mouth of the bay. The bay itself is flat calm. Only minnows dimple its quiet waters. They look like rain drops, a preview of what must inevitably follow.

I have taken the boat to the inlet to dive in one of the deep holes near the barrier beach. Never-ending days of relentless heat have driven thermoclines deep into the bay. Now only these holes contain water cold enough to require a wetsuit.

Underwater I can see the termocline as it stretches out before me, a shimmering interface that separates the warm surface waters from the cooler waters below. Schools of bait fish cruise along the thermocline, for it is a richly productive place.

Competition has become severe. The eelgrass stopped growing as soon as the temperature passed above 68°. The phytoplankton have consumed all the nutrients and are on the wane. Food is becoming scarce at the bottom of the food chain.

The inlet lies near the confluence of two mighty underwater rivers, the Gulf Stream and the Labrador Current. The Gulf Stream surges north carrying warm, clear blue waters and southern fauna. The Labrador Current streams south, its plankton-rich green waters supporting numerous northern species. The bay, influenced by both currents, is the northernmost limit for many southern species and the southernmost limit for many northern species.

Gradually I become aware of an underwater tragedy. Several dead flounder lie white belly up in the shallow water at the edge of the hole. They show no signs of being attacked. They must have fallen victim to an underwater heat wave.

These flounder have succumbed to the ever present danger of climatic fluctuation. An eddy of the Gulf Stream has swirled toward the Cape. In its wake it has left warm tropical waters. The southern beaches of Cape Cod, Nantucket, and Martha's Vineyard are strewn with exotic species. Sargassum weed, Portuguese men-of-war, and colonies of gooseneck barnacles litter the wrack line. In Pleasant Bay, the sun has further heated this water, robbing it of its capacity to hold oxygen. The flounder die first because they lie stationary on the bottom, presenting a wide surface area to the overheated water.

The fish have been dying for three days, and their bodies have attracted numerous sea gulls. I have noticed large well-fed flocks of gulls contentedly squabbling on the rocks and sandspits along the shore. They are probably populations that normally live near the dump, for they evince less fear of man than our own wilder bay gulls.

All sea gulls are opportunistic feeders. They will flock to such an unexpected feast as these flounder. However, they are also specialists. One sea gull will spend most of its time stalking spider crabs, while another treads for quahogs or feeds primarily on horseshoe crabs.

The sea gulls' nesting area is not far from here. Each nest is usually surrounded by the pair's favorite food. One couple has

Winter flounder
(Kenneth R. H. Read)

Gale warnings fly from Chatham light. (William Sargent)

decidedly gourmet tastes. Their nest is surrounded with the scarlet shells of cooked lobsters. Evidently they include the garbage cans of one of Chatham's better restaurants in their feeding territory.

The western sky is filling with an incoming front. Gale warnings fly from Chatham light. A line of beach buggies wends its way back to the motels. The only occupants of the outer beach are the tiny sandpipers that run stiff-leggedly in and out of the backwash in search of bits of food. A red-tailed hawk rides on whisper-like air drafts rising off the dunes. Silhouetted against the graying sky, he sweeps along the dune line on the lookout for birds and voles. I will have to hurry to return to the house before the storm.

Ahead of my boat I notice something white and unnatural floating in the water. Drawing closer, I see it is the grotesque rotting head of an immense tuna. An eel slithers out of its empty eye socket and disappears into the bay.

·The presence of the dead tuna is the result of a minor human deception. A large school of tuna has unexpectedly appeared offshore. Recreational fishermen with little experience are mak-

A storm piles eelgrass along the shore. (William Sargent)

ing as much as $4000 a day fishing for them. If the fishermen can avoid detection, they will not have to purchase an expensive commercial license. Therefore, they clean their catch at sea.

Meanwhile, biologists are unable to get an accurate count and fear that overfishing will decimate the population. It is but another example of what human greed can do to harm the fragile balance of a marine system.

I am speeding through the narrows when the first faint sounds of thunder roll out of the northwestern sky, followed by a blast of wind. Patterns form around the rocks, and wind ripples dance and race across the bay. Soon they have fully engulfed it. I follow the path of still water that curves gracefully down the bay, marking where the channel's different salinity prevents the wind from ruffling its surface.

By dusk I have reached the shore. The wind has picked up. White caps scud across the tops of each wave. The bay is changed — its character now wild and treacherous, its countenance windswept and gray. Gusts of 30- to 40-knot wind blast across the surface. I am on the bluff taking photographs when I notice an overturned sailboat. Its hull wafts crazily back and forth, helpless

66

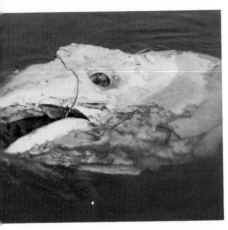

The head of a dead tuna floats in the bay. (William Sargent)

in the choppy water. There is no one aboard, no one trying to right her, no one on the beach. A boat sets out from the far shore. I try to hand signal it toward the stricken vessel. I reason with myself that the sailor has wisely decided not to fight the unconquerable. He must have abandoned ship to wade to shore. Surely he stands there, out of my vision, cursing his ill luck. It is a safe bay, as safe as any body of water short of a bathtub. Even where the boat has capsized it is shallow enough for a person to stand with his head above water. Yet the foreboding grows as the upturned hull continues down its crazy path.

Other boats brave the windswept waters. Emergency lights flash grimly on the far shore. People are dispatched to walk the beaches. We realize we are no longer looking for the man but his body.

The grim truth is revealed the next morning. A flag wafts quietly at half mast. The owner of the sailing camp on the far shore has succumbed to the bay. Curiously, it has been one of the most competent of its habitués that the bay has seen fit to conquer. I log it as a token of respect and hope my passing will be in the clutch of so dear an enemy.

I go down to the beach in the morning to investigate the changes wrought by the storm. The beach has disappeared under a thick

A fishing boat cleans its catch at sea. (Ralph S. MacKenzie)

mat of newly uprooted eelgrass. The mats are crumpled where the high course tide and wind have piled them on the final wrack line. For the next few days the bay will be clear of floating grass.

Grotesque clumps of eelgrass give me an errie feeling. The body of our neighbor who drowned in last night's storm has not been found. He may be lying in just such a thick mat of eelgrass somewhere on the periphery of the bay.

I am distracted from such morbid thoughts by an incongruous sound. Water is gurgling and rushing somewhere along the shore. It is unexpected. The tide and creek normally ascend and descend with a steady quiet regularity. Yet unmistakably there is the sound of falling water.

The high tide has floated a large mat of eelgrass over the marsh. It has settled and collected in the creek, forming a dam. As the tide drops the dam holds. The creek and tidal pond are held a foot higher than usual. Schools of mummichogs and silversides mill about the tiny rivulet trickling over the eelgrass dam. The minnows are unable to ascend the creek to spawn. Millions of eggs will not be laid and will not hatch. It is a tragedy for their population. Inside the creek the eelgrass is starting to stagnate. Fresh water from future rainstorms will lower the salinity, threatening the Spartina.

As I round the corner of the marsh, I see the reason for the noise. Pressure from the water behind the dam has finally broken it. Water surges through the Spartina grass scouring away the sand that protects its roots. A small alluvial fan of gray sand is spreading out across the darker flats. The fan is one inch thick, enough to choke the siphons of clams. The Spartina will die where its roots are exposed. As the tide recedes the alluvial fan spreads itself more thinly across the flats. By low tide it is over.

A rapid change has occurred. The channel of the creek has been altered. Some of the marsh will die. Millions of minnows will not be born. Yet it is a minor tragedy. It will hardly affect the bay. The drowning of our neighbor, though keenly felt by all, will scarcely affect the next town. The Atlantic devoid of bluefin tuna will hardly affect the oceans. And if the oceans were to die? It would hardly effect the stars. Somehow it all seems very important or not so at all.

10. Creek Diving in August

Once I attended a seminar by a well-known ecologist who was conducting pollution studies on salt marshes . . . Without question the speaker was very knowledgeable concerning salt marsh dynamics, but at the same time he seemed to have no feeling about them. He had an immense grasp of energy flows and cycles of matter, but it was obvious that he had never put his head underwater in a salt marsh.

KEN READ, *unpublished manuscript*

It is a lazy August afternoon. The midday sun streams through the front door of the house, suffusing the knotty pine walls with a warm yellow glow. A heavy southwest wind blows up the bay, and flies blunder into the windowpanes. Their buzzing blends harmoniously with the shouts of children sailing on the bay. Sailboats rock gently in the breeze, their halyards beating a rhythmic tattoo against tall metal masts. These are the fleeting days of summer. Soon the same children will drift down long dusty driveways to catch buses to the city and their futures.

There is a comfortable melancholy about the day that drives me from the typewriter. I will take a walk down to the creek where Ken Read and I spent so many summers lying in inches of water, painstakingly photographing every creature living there. Sometimes we would work for three days and shoot hundreds of photographs to get one that we liked. Many photographers shoot through the clear plastic walls of tanks to get their underwater photographs. Undoubtedly it is more efficient but they never experience the exhilaration of finally capturing a hand-held shot of actual behavior occurring in the wild.

In those days, Ken and I would rush to change into our heavy diving gear, for to dawdle on an August marsh is to be plagued by voracious greenheads. The vicious biting flies of the Tabanid genus live their entire life cycle in the marsh. They were quickly attracted to our sweating bodies. Even after we wriggled into our wetsuits we were not safe. Our ankles, hands, and Ken's bald pate remained unprotected. Burdened with hundreds of

The author lies in a tidal creek preparing to photograph. (Kenneth R. H. Read)

pounds of diving and photographic gear, we slogged across the marsh to the blessed refuge of the shallow creek.

Underwater, problems of heat and greenheads blissfully disappeared. Cool green waters rippled over the sun-dappled bottom, and eelgrass waved in the current of the outgoing tide. Spartina stalks jutted out of the sides of the steep peat banks that rose on either side of us.

Inch-long marsh shrimp glided over the bottom and swam up to grasp the Spartina blades. Stalked invertebrate eyes from a distant past gazed into our own. Mechanical-looking appendages probed and whirred as they worked over black fronds of decaying eelgrass.

We could see tiny black particles of eelgrass through the transparent sides of the shrimp. The stomach convulsively kneaded the particles and passed them on to the intestines. The shrimp was actually not digesting the eelgrass, only stripping off the nutritious coating of microorganisms: bacteria, fungi, and protozoa that were in the process of decomposing the plant matter.

The shrimp and other detritus feeders are important links in the food chain that transfers the sun's energy caught by the

71

The egg mass of an isopod
parasitizing a shrimp.
(Kenneth R. H. Read)

Silversides stare apprehensively at
our intrusion. (Kenneth R. H. Read)

Minnows and mudsnails approach
the bait. (Kenneth R. H. Read)

marsh plants to the fish, birds, and mammals that live in the bay and ocean beyond. Like most water-living creatures, these shrimp were highly parasitized. The gill chambers of many of them bulged with masses of eggs. The eggs looked as though they could have belonged to the shrimp, but they were actually laid by a huge isopod parasite that lived within the shrimp's exoskeleton.

Many of the shrimp carried leeches, which feed off animals in the water. The shrimp were about an inch long, the leeches an eighth of an inch. We were able to obtain hand-held photographs of the minute penis of the leech.

We often used bait to attract the droves of minnows that surged up the creek. This was easily obtained by plucking a ribbed mussel (*Modiolus demissus*) that proliferated in the peat. They are filter feeders that grow in profusion on the rich supply of plankton flowing by with the tide. The water also contains large quantities of inedible detritus, which they eject in clumps of mucus and mud called pseudofeces. They produce large quantities of pseudofeces that build the marsh higher. The mussels themselves have to keep moving up the marsh to avoid being buried by their own by-products.

We crushed the fragile mussels and spread them on the bottom. The mummichogs (*Fundulus heteroclitus*) swarmed in instantly. Day after day the same minnow grabbed the bait and skipped across the surface in a vain attempt to outswim his pursuers. All but the largest chubs rushed in, unmindful of our flashing strobe, to tear into the bait. Transparent silversides (*Menidia menidia*) hesitantly approached and held themselves in the current, like barracuda. They peered at us apprehensively while elegantly gleaning tiny scraps of bait stirred up from the voracious feeding of the mummichogs below.

Sheepshead minnows (*Cyprinodon variegatus*) accompanied the mummichogs, nipping aggressively at their flanks. Soon we were engulfed in a Lilliputian feeding frenzy. Huge mummichog faces loomed into the frames of our cameras and shrimp swarmed over our hands, drawn by the lingering taint of the bait. The ticklish attentions of their tiny chelipedes would distract us from our photography.

The odor of the bait also attracted armies of mud snails (*Nasarrius obsoletus*). They approached from downstream following the scent with outstretched proboscises. Gliding resolutely toward the bait, they looked like phalanxes of Hannibal's elephants charging in for an attack. Within fifteen minutes they would transform the bait into a twisting, tumbling mass of gastropods. We removed them upstream where they couldn't detect the scent, but they were always replaced by a seemingly endless supply from the waters below.

Finally, spider crabs (*Libinia libinia*) emerged and tried to haul the entire broken shell under the peat bank where they could enjoy their meal without the annoyance of the minnows and mud snails.

The feast inevitably ended with the appearance of an eighteen-inch eel (*Anguilla rosrata*) that lived in a hole in the peat. It would glide into a piece of algae and poke its head out to glower at us. We were able to obtain excellent photographs of the lateral-line pits that dot its upper and lower jaws. The lateral lines are used to detect vibrations in the water, allowing the nocturnal animal to locate food and avoid danger in the dark.

Suddenly the eel forged in to engulf the entire bait with one violent convulsion. Then we realized it was eyeing our hands. We quickly plunged them into the bottom to remove the odor of the mussel blood we had used as bait. I would not care to be bleeding and unable to get out of the water when there are eels around.

The glowering presence of the eel always ended the day. The swarms of minnows gradually dissolved into a discreet few, and the creek quieted down. The tide had drained the pond, leaving only a few inches of slack water remaining on the bottom. It would be time to leave this exotic miniature world.

The gentle warmth of the sun's last rays was always a welcome treat from the lingering chill of the dive. After we hauled our heavy equipment back across the marsh we would stretch out on the soft cushion of dry eelgrass to enjoy the sunset.

It was on one of those days that we witnessed the departure of the terns. A new front of cool air was arriving from the west, clearing the sky of clouds. The setting sun tore a hole through the bottom of the rolling gray mass of storm clouds. A shaft of light suddenly illuminated a huge flock of terns. The sky was white with them. Their breasts glistened with the light. Graceful swept-back wings and forked tails stood out in vivid contrast against the steel-gray clouds. For the next hour we watched as wave after wave of them flew silently overhead. The following night there were a few; then there were none.

It was a sign. The raucous calls of terns would no longer dominate the bay. The summer visitors were silently slipping away. The bay was preparing for the serious business of autumn.

Year after year the terns arrive before the solstice and depart before the equinox. Their migrations always occur within a few days of the anniversary of the year before. The changing length of daylight is the cue that initiates their departure. They cannot afford to leave exactly on the equinox, the day when the hours of daylight and dark are equal. The fledgling chicks must still be fed on the schools of sand eels and silversides. These schools must also move south, but their migration is triggered by water temperature. By leaving before the equinox the terns ensure that they leave before their food source disappears. We can only marvel at the complex biological clocks that faithfully empty and fill the bay of its inhabitants at the same time each year. They, of course, may marvel at the regularity of our leaving, year after year on Labor Day — three weeks before the equinox.

Canadian geese (Ralph S. MacKenzie)

Autumn

Autumn comes to the sea with a fresh blaze of phosphorescence, when every wave crest is aflame. Here and there the whole surface may glow with sheets of cold fire, while below schools of fish pour through the water like molten metal.

RACHEL CARSON, *The Sea Around Us*

11. Indian Summer

When the female blue crab is ready, she opens her newly shaped abdomen to expose two genital pores. Into these the male inserts his pleopods or two small appendages underneath the tip of his elongated abdominal apron. When all is in place, the female so extends her abdomen that it folds around and over the male's back, thus effectively preventing any risk of coitus interruptus. Truly blue crabs are locked in love's embrace.

WILLIAM W. WARNER, *Beautiful Swimmers*

Labor Day passes and the bay reverts to a more serious mien. Gone are the frivolous boats of summer, replaced by the sturdy workboats of autumn. I recognize their clean simple lines as old friends; the green boat pulls eelpots; the white boat dredges for scallops; the black one hunts the horseshoe crab.

The waning days of summer marked the inexorable passage of the seasons toward the autumnal equinox. There were fewer hours of sunlight to warm the bay. Gradually the surface waters cooled and plunged to the bay floor. Though reminiscent of spring this autumn overturn was less exuberant than its vernal counterpart.

The bay is strangely empty now — the season at slack tide. The midday sun is gloriously warm, and the ocean retains the heat of summer. This is Indian summer, a brief reprieve from winter.

The upper reaches of the bay are the best places to enjoy Indian summer. The ponds hold the heat of summer and life proceeds at a leisurely pace. People swarm to the rivers and ponds where the winter flounder have just arrived. Cape Codders who haven't seen their neighbors all summer count on these days to become reacquainted and to fill their freezers for winter. Unlike in spring, the flounders' flesh is now firm, their bellies full of next year's generation.

Undoubtedly the Nauset and Monomoyick Indians derived as much pleasure as we do from this season, which is thought to

The last boat of summer
(William Sargent)

79

have received its name from the time after the crops had been harvested and the Indians were free to enjoy a brief moment of warmth before the winter freeze. It was during this time that they speared flounders, dug quahogs, and caught blue crabs.

Indian summer is still the best time to catch blue crabs, and one of the best places is in Lonnie's River, the small river we visited during the spring herring run. Now all the herring fingerlings have spilled down the fish ladder into the bay to repeat the great cycle of their species.

The river teems with "snapper blues," immature bluefish about six inches long. They have come here to feed on the herring. Mercilessly they herd and slash into the schools, leaving maimed fingerlings in their wake. Needlefish, southern visitors who appear in the bay in August and September, lurk in the shallows. Occasionally one will lunge out like a miniature barracuda to capture a silverside minnow.

The banks of the river are overgrown with tall, lush stands of cordgrass, topped with spiky seed-filled heads. Each puff of wind dislodges a few seeds that will float around the bay until they find a suitable place to lodge and flourish.

Some crows derisively call out their displeasure at my intrusion. Wary lookout birds sit in the highest cedar trees, scrutinizing my every move. Glimpses of brilliant blue flash through the leaves as a flock of bluejays screech through the forest. Their calls seem alien to the scene. I always associate them with the deep inner woods. A kingfisher plunges from his perch on an overhanging branch. He emerges from the shallows with a stunned mummichog in his bill. He emits a victorious rattling cry, turns the minnow, and swallows it head first.

A green heron fishes with an ingenious lure. He drops a small piece of grass into the current and flies downstream below it. As the piece of grass rounds the bend the heron peers intently at it. An inquisitive minnow rises to investigate the lure. The heron's snakelike neck strikes out and returns with the unsuspecting minnow in its bill.

The water is exceptionally clear. It is twenty minutes before low tide. During the ebb, cool, clear pond waters flush the turbidity back into the bay. When the tide turns the murkiness will return with it.

The deep channel that runs down the center of the river is a jumbled array of color. The brilliant reds and yellows of sponges intermix with the deep green of codium and the fragile pinks of hydroids. Schools of minnows flash like silver shadows through the upthrust fingers of a brilliantly colored red-beard sponge (*Microciona prolifera*). An old quahog shell is covered with curious

A dead bluefish floats on the river.
(Ralph S. MacKenzie)

yellow protrusions, the toadstool-shaped current openings of the boring sponge (*Clione celata*).

Clione plays an important role as an agent in returning calcium carbonate to the water of the bay. It attacks shellfish by honeycombing their calcareous shells with filaments, which secrete an acid that bores tiny holes in their shells. The shell becomes covered with a delicate filagree of golden tracings. Eventually the entire shell decomposes, and only a large bright-yellow sponge remains.

The colorful green fingers of *Codium fragile* are anchored to the shell of a living scallop. Codium is a recent inhabitant of the bay. The colorful but unwanted green algae was accidentally introduced to the East Coast in 1957. Spores of the algae probably came to this coast on the shells of oysters from Japan or Europe. Now they have become a well-established nuisance in the bay. Their habit of attaching to the shells of mollusks leads to great destruction. Storms tear both codium and shellfish from the bottom and throw them on the beach, where they decompose.

Tucked between some of the sponges are clumps of what look like filamentous red algae. On closer inspection, they are revealed to be a delicate colony of the hydroid (*Obelia commissuralis*), flowerlike animals that sway gracefully in the ebbing tide. They stretch out tentacles to snag the plankton that drifts by with the current. The tentacles are armed with nematocysts, vicious stinging cells that paralyze their prey.

The fragile pink colony is a teeming jungle of miniature life. Caprellid shrimp reach into the current with ungainly looking claws. Bobbing and weaving in the swift water, they are elaborately equipped with Dr. Seusslike appendages to snare their planktonic prey.

A transparent sea spider gingerly crawls over the bushy terrain. Occasionally it launches itself into the water, flailing all eight legs in a frantic effort to gain the next perch. Nudibranches — shell-less snails — browse on the hydroid colony. They are able to ingest the stinging cells of the hydroids without the cells' discharging. The cells then migrate to the surface of the nudibranches, where they erupt through the skin. The still undischarged nematocysts then become part of the nudibranches' own defense.

I have dug my hand into the soft bottom sediments in order to hold my place against the current. My hand grasps a forgotten relic of days long gone. It is the nine-inch shell of an oyster (*Crassostrea virginica*). Oysters used to proliferate here. The Indian shell mounds that ring the bay consist largely of their remains. During the thirties truckloads of Pleasant Bay oysters

A heron watches for minnows. (Ralph S. MacKenzie)

were shipped to Haymarket in Boston and the Fulton Fish Market in New York.

Oyster beds were particularly concentrated in the brackish ponds and rivers that drained into the bay. The fresh water helped protect them from starfish and oyster drills that can only live in the saltier waters of the lower bay. The oyster drill (*Urosalpinx cinerea*) is a half-inch snail that rasps a neat hole through the shell of the oyster and consumes the contents. Its tool is a radula, a toothed tongue that gouges out the hole after another special organ has secreted acid into the shell.

The radula and the strong pulling arms of the starfish are

formidable weapons for the oyster to contend with. Natural selection could have eventually evolved oysters with a different anatomy to combat these weapons. Instead a short cut was taken. They have evolved a behavioral repertoire that includes producing millions of offspring that can swim, which gives them a better chance of settling in an area safe from these predators.

First the adult oyster releases over 100 million eggs at once. It has been estimated that if all the offspring from one female oyster were to survive, in five generations they would require a volume 250 times that of the earth.

The immature oysters then remain part of the plankton community for a fortnight. Initially, the tiny plankters are swept in and out with every tide. Soon, however, they start to descend to the bottom during ebb tide and ascend into the currents during flood tide. Gradually this behavior causes them to be carried up the bay and into the freshwater ponds.

The best place for immature oysters to settle is on the shells of adult oysters. Thick beds of them used to surround the freshwater springs in these ponds. The larvae were attracted to the oyster beds by ectocrines released from living oysters. As many as 670 immature oysters, or spat, might settle on one square inch of adult oyster shell.

The oyster fishery ended in the forties and fifties, when most of the creeks were dredged to allow motorboats access to the ponds. It is theorized that before the creeks were dredged each incoming high tide would transport a lens of warm salt water into each pond. The greater density of this saline-rich layer of warm water would cause it to plunge through the colder fresh water where the adult oysters lived. The rapid rise in temperature caused the adult oysters to spawn. Thus, each pond acted like a natural propagation laboratory to replenish the bay's crop of oysters.

Oysters are one of the most profligate of species. They release billions of eggs when they spawn. Their profligacy reminds us of the moon jellies encountered in this same river in spring. Unlike the moon jellies, who reproduce both sexually and asexually, oysters reproduce by sex alone. What can they tell us about that most significant step in evolution from asexual to fully sexual reproduction?

If we look at their situation perhaps we can understand more about the evolution of sexual reproduction. We might also gain some insight into why humans have inherited this form of reproduction. For if there were not advantages to sex, it would not have evolved and we would still reproduce by cloning.

In a situation of extreme competition for a limited amount of space any advantage can be crucial. This is the case with oysters. Only one immature oyster out of the hundreds that settle on a shell will survive. If one of these inherits an advantage, like the ability to develop a harder shell or grow more quickly, it may be the sole survivor.

Sexual reproduction is a favorable strategy because it hastens evolution by allowing an animal to mix genes. This increases the chances that a favorable trait will emerge.

An analogy can be made with gambling strategies. In an unchanging environment asexual reproduction is a sure bet. In a changing environment it can be a sure loss. Sexual reproduction becomes a better gambling strategy because it allows nature to hedge her bets. Let's go back to the oysters.

On the oyster bed competition is severe and mortality is high. Only one larval oyster out of the hundreds that settle on a shell will survive. If they reproduced asexually oysters could only rear clones with all the same traits. None of the clones would have a different trait that could make it the sole survivor.

Sexual reproduction allows the oyster to hedge its bets. By mixing genes oysters can produce a variety of offspring with different traits. One of these traits may give one of the offspring an advantage that will allow it to become the sole survivor on the oyster shell.

If an environment changes so that competition is reduced and more offspring survive, the advantage could swing back to asexual reproduction. Some people argue that humans have such control over their environment that it has become less of a factor in our evolution. Does this mean that we might do better to reproduce asexually?

A nudibranch feeds on a hydroid colony. (Wes Pratt)

84

It has been argued that asexual reproduction, if it could get a start, would be so advantageous that it would replace sexual reproduction in most vertebrates including humans. In fact, the few fish and amphibians that have re-evolved asexual reproduction are all exclusively asexual. Fortunately evolution needs some preadaptations or raw materials with which to work. It might also be advantageous for us to have gills or wings, but we lack the raw material to evolve them.

As mammals we have moved far beyond the invertebrate ancestor that set us on the track of exclusive sexual reproduction. We seem to be stuck with sex and only a disgruntled few regret it. However, should asexual reproduction ever emerge among humans it might indeed enjoy a selective advantage; then sex and men would be superfluous.

Blue crabs are starting to appear along the shallow edges of the river. They are at their feistiest in late August and September. It is the breeding season and they are irritable and more territorial than usual. Two males with colorful claws jab and feint at each other like pugnacious boxers. The color of their claws was partly responsible for the location of New York City. The explorer De Vries noticed blue crabs along the shores of the Hudson River. He noted them "to be of a very good taste, their claws are the color of the flag of our prince; orange, white and blue so that the crabs show sufficiently that we ought to people the country and that it belongs to us." It is not recorded what the Indians thought of this reasoning.

At the entrance of the pond the river shoals to a shallow bank. Here the crabs are performing their biological imperative. A male has spotted a female. He rears up on the very tips of his walking legs. It is what animal behaviorists call an intention movement. It is a ritualized exaggeration of the same movement he will later use to "cradle" her.

He extends his claws and starts sensuously to whirl his swimming legs. She is mesmerized by his display. She starts to rock back and forth to his rhythm. Thus assured, the male approaches, still whirling his hypnotic legs. It is a critical moment. He lashes out and grabs her. She responds submissively, and he is able to position her safely under him. They are now in what is termed the "cradle carry."

He will hold her gently for the next few days until she moults. It is only then that mating can occur. The long cradle carry is another instance of an elaborate behavior that has evolved to ensure reproductive success. It provides excellent protection for the female during her critical final moult. More importantly, it ensures that the male will be present during the crucially short period after her moult when she can receive him. Biologists agree that, without this behavior, the species would certainly perish.

The female's moult lasts two hours. Finally she lies exhausted but triumphant in her glistening new shell. The male allows her a few moments to rest and swallow some water. The water will swell her tissues to fill out her full body size. The male then helps her turn over so she lies beneath him. Gently and patiently the lovemaking begins. They will remain blissfully locked in a lovers' embrace for the next five to twelve hours. After they have finished he cradles her for another forty-eight hours until her shell hardens.

She will not use his sperm packet until the spring. In May she will start developing an orange egg mass called sponge. By then she will have returned to the saltier deep waters of the lower bay. The egg mass will start to assume a darker, more caviar-like appearance. Finally small zoea, or larval crabs, are hatched. They float with the plankton near the surface. It is during this time that they can be killed by lowered salinity from a rainstorm or be swept out to sea. All is not lost, however, if they are swept out to sea. Not only can the immature crabs survive in the ocean, but it seems to be their normal means of dispersal.

This piece of scientific minutiae, a mere footnote in biological research, is taken very seriously on the bay, where Indian-summer blue crabbing is an earnest occupation. People used to assume that the offspring of blue crabs mainly came from the adult population in the bay. If there were a lot of adult crabs one year they would expect plentiful crabs in following years. Now, however, biologists are starting to learn that immature crabs are long distance travelers.

Most of the crab larvae that arrive in Pleasant Bay are born in southern estuaries like Chesapeake Bay. Thus, the weather in the Chesapeake or the vagaries of the Gulf Stream could help account for the rapid fluctuations of crabs in such northern areas as Pleasant Bay. This system of dispersal seems to be very effective: there is a population of blue crab off the coast of Israel that appears to have been accidentally carried there from their normal range on the East Coast of the United States.

It has been another long day. The setting sun casts a golden hue on the shore. Delicate aster blossoms grace the upper marsh where the slender stems of salt marsh hay will soon topple before the autumn winds. They will leave the upper marsh a tussle of russet cowlicks. Walking across them will be like walking on the back of an immense shaggy animal.

Spawning oysters
(Chesapeake Biological Laboratory)

A male blue crab (William Sargent)

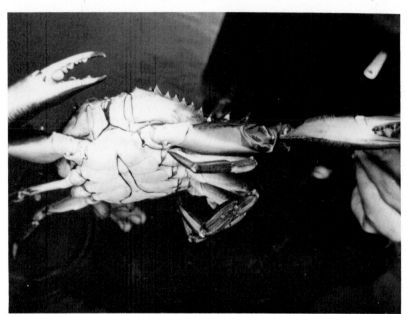

A blue crab courting display
(Kenneth R. H. Read)

12. Autumn Eeling

You get all slimed up as though you skun a kegful.

PHIL SCHWIND, *Making a Living Alongshore*

We just missed another hurricane. The Cape has not suffered a serious hurricane since I was a boy and the Coast Guard had to launch a boat off our beach in order to rescue some neighbors stranded on Payson's Island. Fine old trees have grown too high, boathouses have been built too close to the water, and piers stretch too far out into the bay. Everyone says the next hurricane will do great damage, but it hasn't hit yet.

This latest hurricane passes through as a downgraded tropical storm. In its wake it leaves an ominous stillness. The sky is breathless and yellow. The bay is already full. Water laps the bottoms of the bluffs and fields. Will it ever stop its rise?

The bay has already flooded the marsh, and drowned the salt hay meadows. The marsh looks as it did two generations ago when it was still open water.

Great schools of fish are riffling the bay's surface. There is something strange about their behavior. Terns fly over them, then seem to lose interest. Something frightens the fish. The entire school makes a mad rush to the surface. Fusiform bodies leap clear of the water trying to escape whatever it is that is feeding on them from below.

Hundreds of yellow tails slice through the water. The entire school is churning around in a wide arc. Their swimming has stirred up the bottom, and loose pieces of red algae swirl to the surface. Assured that they are indeed menhaden, locally called pogies, I slip into the turbid water where silver flashes mark the fishes' presence. Many have great gashes torn from their throats, a certain sign that bluefish have been feeding on them.

It is too turbid for underwater photography, so I continue down the bay. Other people have found more schools. I talk to a boy who is snagging them on the treblehook of a surface plug.

Menhaden (M. J. Reeber)

"Whatcha catchin'?" "Manhattan," he replies. Quite a thing to catch I felt. "Gonna eat 'em?" "Naw, they ain't worth anythin'." He is right, of course. Given the choice, who could stomach "Manhattan"?

He meant to say "menhaden," but *Brevoortia tyrannus* go by a multitude of pseudonyms. They make up the largest commercial fishery on the East Coast. This oily fish of the herring family is favored bait for lobster fishermen and longliners.

The prime use of the fish, however, is to be ground into a fish protein concentrate for fertilizer, soaps, and poultry food. The demand for menhaden is so great that Crisfield, a small town on Chesapeake Bay where most of the country's menhaden are landed, ranks as the third largest fishing port on the East Coast.

Most of the fishmeal is trucked to Maryland's large chicken farms where it is used as poultry feed. One of the reasons that chicken is a relatively inexpensive food in this country is that they are fed on menhaden. Chickens grow rapidly on fish meal and can be quickly converted into human food. The efficiency of the industry is largely dependent on menhaden's unique ability to convert plankton directly into fish protein. In most other food chains, the nutrients would have to pass through other intermediate organisms — zooplankton and smaller fish — before they would be incorporated into a medium-size fish like the menhaden.

Blue heron congregate on a small hummock of Spartina grass in the shallow waters of the sandflats; the shoals prevent outboard motors from approaching too close to disturb them. The wind blows my boat toward the hummock, where I can photograph the skittish birds.

The water is dropping quickly. I hope the wind will carry me to the channel before I go aground. The outboard is useless, but the wind blows me rapidly toward a large green work boat. The fisherman looks like a young Huck Finn in a floppy straw hat. The herons have flown so I start photographing the operation. As I draw nearer I realize that the fisherman is a woman.

Her boat is already aground. It is too heavy to move so we will have to wait out the tide. The situation is not unpleasant. The sun is warm, the water is clear, her background interesting.

She told me she had been a craftswoman on the lower East Side of Manhattan. She decided that fishing was a noble way to make a living and moved to the Cape to take up the trade. She caught all her own bait, tended her traps, and made fifty to one hundred dollars a day. She loved the freedom and was very good company. We agreed that even with minor frustrations

A great blue heron (William Sargent)

such as going aground in mid-bay the lifestyle beat nine-to-five in an office.

In the deep channel, just beyond our grounded boats, discrete paths can be seen through the eelgrass. They are clues that the eels have started one of nature's most spectacular migrations — a pilgrimage to certain death in the cold, murky depths of the Atlantic.

Large black-and-silver eels have started to move down the bay. Every night throughout October and November, thousands of them will slither through the eelgrass toward the waiting Atlantic. Their eyes have become enlarged, and they have ceased feeding. They may never feed again.

They are sexually mature adult eels, resplendent in their newly acquired courtship colors. Their backs have turned blacker and their flanks and bellies have a silvery sheen. The males are eight to ten years old; the females are twice as large and slightly older.

They have left the freshwater ponds and streams to push toward the Atlantic. Some have traveled overland, crawling snakelike through dew-drenched grasslands. They have slithered across marshes and swum down creeks. Before so many of the marshes were ditched for mosquito control, fishermen built fykes (wooden lathe traps set into the marshes) to interrupt the migration.

At the inlet the eels will once again enter the marine world. From the fjords of Scandinavia, the ponds of Europe, and the bays of America millions of their sleek serpentine bodies have been drawn as if by a magnet to the inky depths of the Sargasso Sea, south of Bermuda.

In an underwater ritual we can only imagine, millions of slithering eel bodies will unite to spawn and die. The Atlantic will then be filled with billions of leptocephali, their paper-thin transparent offspring. Finely veined with delicate spines, they look like animate elm leaves. So dissimilar are they from adult eels, scientists originally thought they were a separate species.

Billions of the delicate animals are swept along in the gentle grip of the Gulf Stream. They flow passively toward the bays and lagoons their parents left years ago. Their bodies continue to change. By the time they reach the inlet some will have metamorphosed to elvers three to four inches long and capable of swimming.

Many of their brethren, the offspring of European eels, will not have changed, for theirs must be a longer journey. Entrusted to the constancy of ocean currents, they must remain a part of the slowly drifting plankton community for as long as three years.

By next April, tens of thousands of transparent "glass eels" will have entered the bay, to start their adult nocturnal existence. Their skins will darken to complement the herring battling beside them in the runs. They will have completed another cycle that locks the bay to the ocean and the seasons to the year. Out of one of nature's deadliest pilgrimages will have emerged tiny vital threads of life, ready to do battle to perpetuate their species.

The common eel
(Kenneth R. H. Read)

Tending eelpots (William Sargent)

13. A Day in Mid-Bay

The veliger's a lively tar, the liveliest afloat,
A whirling wheel on either side propels his little boat;
But when the danger signal warns his bustling submarine,
He stops the engine, shuts the port, and drops below unseen.

W. GARSTANG, *"The Ballad of the Veliger," The Open Sea*

The sun hangs low in the crisp cobalt air of autumn, spreading a flickering path of silver across the bay. Zephyrs of cool ocean air pile tiny puffs of cumulus clouds above the dune line on the outer beach.

It is dead low tide. Shoal water stretches out interminably in all directions. I am in the middle of the bay but could wade to shore in almost any direction. The only sure feature of the bottom is Crooked Channel, the remains of a glacial river that wends its tortuous path through the shallow waters. The Dry Hump, a tiny island of sand, emerges briefly only at low tide. I have come out here to check on some quahogs I planted with some students several years ago.

Slight wisps of early morning mist curled about our legs, and the sun made exaggerated silhouettes of our toiling forms. Armed with clam rakes and bushel baskets, we looked like a scene from the romantic past. We hoped we were part of the changing face of Pleasant Bay.

We had been experimenting with several types of aquaculture. Each group of four students tended its own underwater plot. The plots were marked off and contained different-sized quahogs (*Mercenaria mercenaria*).

I am able to locate the plot of parent stock. Their dark feeding siphons are extended above the sand to filter the rich autumn plankton blooms. Some of them were dredged from polluted waters near Boston. After a few months of filtering the clean bay waters they cleansed themselves and released spat. Now their stomachs are becoming pink and rotund. They have lost the mealy taste they acquire when spawning.

The sun silhouettes a quahogger.
(*Cape Cod Times* Photo by Milton Moore)

93

Other plots contained immature quahogs that had started life in a laboratory. When we bought them they were about a quarter of an inch in diameter. Those that were planted at that size fared poorly, but those that we transferred to floating rafts survived and grew rapidly. By the end of summer they were one inch across. We planted them in October and November when most of their predators had left the bay but when the substrate was still soft enough for the young quahogs to dig in for the winter.

In this country, aquaculture is a young science. It has reached sophisticated levels in the Far East, particularly in China. Cape Cod has indulged in an incipient form of aquaculture since the War of 1812. Perhaps "aquaculture" is too elegant a term to apply to behavior that could also be termed grand larceny. Oyster stocks had declined in Cape Cod waters through a combination of overfishing and disease. Yankee schooners started to sail south to dredge in Rhode Island, Connecticut, New York, and New Jersey, setting off a dangerous chain reaction that depleted the oyster beds all along the coast.

Finally they settled into what was called the "Virginia Trade," the practice of dredging Chesapeake Bay oysters for "embedding" in New England waters. After the transplanted oysters had picked up the saltier taste of northern waters, they could be lucratively marketed as Cotuit or Wellfleet oysters.

This practice was eventually modified to become a means of rebuilding the New England breeding stocks. Of course, many of the undersized oysters found their way to ready markets.

Planting quahogs (*The Cape Codder*)

Big Pleasant Bay (*The Cape Codder*)

It is not known whether the practice actually helped start the Civil War, but it is known that the war helped to end it. It flourished briefly after the end of the war, then collapsed when the Chesapeake watermen developed their own indigenous industry. At its peak the Virginia trade was producing five times what the Chesapeake now provides and more than double today's national consumption of oysters.

Management of the shell fisheries was turned over to Massachusetts towns in 1945. Only since 1975 have they received federal and state funds to develop sophisticated management and aquaculture techniques.

One area indicates how productive the entire bay could become. On almost any day of the year except in the dead of winter, fifteen to twenty boats can be seen scattered over as many acres of water. The only sound that can be heard is the quiet scraping of long-handled bull rakes as fishermen work them through the bottom.

Each fisherman has a rake custom-built for him by a single craftsman who supplies most of Cape Cod. He makes six different kinds of rakes for different bottom conditions, ranging from muddy to sandy. The work is back breaking. The rakes

95

The only sound is the quiet scraping of the bull rakers. (*Cape Cod Times* Photo by Milton Moore)

have a fifteen-foot handle and a large, heavy wire basket for holding the quahogs. The raker tosses the head of the rake away from his boat. Then he grasps the handle and retrieves the rake with a series of back-breaking jerks. The jerks work the teeth of the rake through the bottom.

A good raker can tell by the feel of the rake if the teeth are hitting little necks, cherry stones, or chowders. Those are the three market sizes that determine how much he can expect to get paid for his labor.

The area where the bull rakers work has enjoyed three natural sets since 1935. A set occurs when a large number of free-floating larval shellfish settle to the bottom in one spot. The latest set occurred in 1965. Since then over a million dollars' worth of quahogs have come out of this fifteen-acre area of water. A good set of scallops can yield that amount of money in a few weeks. Even fishing for the lowly conch can yield a fisherman $46,000 for the 25-week season. Clearly shellfish are valuable resources

96

that can be greatly increased by proper management and aqua-culture techniques. The rich shallow waters of Pleasant Bay could be a valuable food source for the future.

The bay has supported fishermen for hundreds of years. Many of the former fisheries have disappeared with the oysters. "Tur-tlin'" used to be one of the mainstays of the bay. The bay is the northernmost limit of the succulent diamondback terrapin. Fish-ermen used to spread nets across many of the creeks and inlets to trap hundreds of animals. "Old Timers" recall watching fish-ermen barrel and ship fifteen hundred turtles a day to Boston to supply the gourmet food trade. Now it is a rarity to see a terrapin on the bay. This summer I did see one adult and came across many nests pilfered by skunks and raccoons. I hope some will survive and the former population will build again. If it does, may we have the sense not to overexploit a population already diminished by living on the margin of its range.

Another organism that is a far greater threat to the shellfish industry is a single-celled microscopic species of plankton, *Gon-yaulax tamerensis*. It is responsible for what shellfishermen fear most: the red tide.

Red tides occur in the spring and fall when the water temper-ature is between 50° and 60° Fahrenheit (10° and 16° Centigrade),

A diamondback terrapin
(William Sargent)

97

which is when the animals break out of their tiny seedlike cysts that protect them in the winter. During a red tide the water becomes saturated with toxins released by the gonyaulax organism. The paralytic toxins are so strong that the CIA has investigated using them as rapid-acting poisons for James Bond–type political assassinations. A small amount of the toxin can be put into a dart that is shot into the victim, causing him to die of a heart attack. The toxins are virtually undetectable, so that after the dart is removed there is no evidence that he did not suffer a natural attack.

In the bay shellfish ingest the red-tide organisms when they eat. They eat by filtering water and plankton into their gut. This method of feeding also accumulates large quantities of the toxins in their body tissues. The shellfish are only slightly affected by the toxins, but people who eat them become violently ill and can die.

The gonyaulax species are recent arrivals to the bay. They are northern species that used to be restricted to colder northern waters by the Cape Cod barrier. It is believed that a 1972 hurricane was responsible for flushing the organism south to gain a foothold in the bay. Now that they have established themselves in the bay's brackish ponds, it is unlikely that they will disappear.

The thick-walled cysts can remain in the sediments of these ponds for two years without feeding. When conditions are just right they break out of their cysts, and large blooms of them are flushed into the bay, where they infect the shellfish beds.

Fresh water seems to be a critical environmental factor in producing the blooms for they usually occur after a heavy rainstorm. Some scientists have speculated that fertilizers in runoff rainwater might provide the nutrients for recent massive blooms.

It has been a long day on the flats. The tide has risen and fallen again. Soon we will get a cold snap and the temperature will start to drop in earnest. The dogfish and sea robins will hasten to the inlet to start their migration south. The crabs will move into the deep channels, where they can bury themselves in the mud for the winter. The quahogs will retract their siphons and dig farther into the sand. I will hang up my diving gear until spring.

14. The Blue-Eyed Scallop

The hard part of scalloping is shucking. I always get slowed down by anatomy lessons.

PHIL SCHWIND, *Making a Living Alongshore*

A swimming scallop
(Kenneth R. H. Read)

The fluted patterns of the two-year-old scallop (Ralph S. MacKenzie)

The bay is cloaked in a cold wet blanket of fog that obliterates the shore and chills the soul. My world is constricted to a boat length of visibility in a vaporous gray void. A gust of wind ruffles the surface. The fog rolls on. A hole appears in the gossamer blanket. For an instant, I see I am surrounded by a fleet of small boats. Enshrouded in fog, they toil to haul heavy dredges across the bay floor. They glide through gray vapors like ghostly apparitions. Skeletal outlines of makeshift rigs arch over each boat, and dark hooded men bend over the culling boards. There is no time to ponder the scene. With frightening speed the fog rolls in again and engulfs the fleet. It mutes our voices. We travel together again, each boat alone in its own gray world.

It is October 1, the first day of the scalloping season. Commercial fishermen have been looking forward to this day. Throughout the summer they have been working long hard hours on the offshore fisheries. Now the weather is beginning to change, the easterlies starting to blow.

If the scallops are plentiful, commercial fishermen can look forward to making a good living at the inshore fisheries. The quiet waters of the bay will be a welcome relief from the pounding white water of Georges Bank.

In the bars and tackle shops there has been endless speculation about the outlook for the season. Bullrakers are consulted for advice. These commercial quahog fishermen have been on the bay all summer. They have had a chance to locate areas where scallops are concentrated. Some say Crooked Channel and Dogfish Bar look promising. The common flats might be all right after a good storm clears away the weed.

It is the season for speculation. Fishermen start sounding like

The bay was cloaked in a cold wet blanket of fog. (*The Cape Codder*)

commodities traders with a saltier point of view: "I dunno, market's been down on shoestrings and it don't look too good for winkles, eithah. I might jist stick with them piss clams for awhile and wait to see if the market don't go up in December before riggin' for scallops."

After the scalloper swings the dredge over the side and empties his catch, the culling board is a mixed array of eelgrass, mud, empty shells, crabs, worms, fish, and scallops. Great balls of fresh eelgrass gleam in the sun. Eels and flounders slither down the board, and green crabs nip at the fishermen's fingers.

Concentrated fishing for scallops does not imperil future stocks. Fortunately, bay scallops (*Aequipecten irradians*) are ideally suited by nature to benefit from simple management techniques. The scallops occur in two distinct sizes: The one-year-olds are one inch across and the two-year-olds are over two inches across.

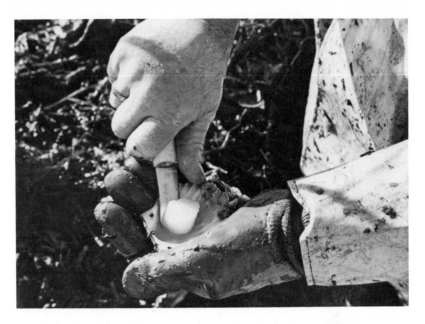

Shucking scallops (*The Cape Codder*)

The raised ridge of their first winter clearly stands out along the colorful fluted pattern of the two-year shell. Culling is easy. The first-year scallops are returned, the second-year ones retained.

The two-year-old scallops spawned during the summer. They will not survive the winter, so fishermen can harvest all of them without depleting next year's crop.

Harvesting the scallops is the easy part. The real work will come later, in the shucking houses. The only salable part of the scallop is the large abductor muscle that controls the shells. The shuckers have to cut the top of the muscle, flip away the shell, clean out the gurry, and sever the bottom of the muscle. This is accomplished in a series of rapid motions. The cleaned muscles, called eyes, are tossed into plastic quart containers. A good shucker can clean nine pounds of scallops in an hour.

Scallops tend to congregate in autumn. No one knows exactly how or why they do this. During the summer they are scattered randomly throughout the bay. They can move by using their large abductor muscle to snap their two shells together, which forces water out of their body cavity and causes the scallops to skip up off the bottom. By using their body organs to force the water out in different directions they can effectively control their movement.

Some people claim to have seen acres of scallops using this method to move up the bay at night. Starfish are also known to migrate in autumn. They do this because less fresh water flows into the bay so that the salinity level no longer restricts them to the lower bay. It is possible that the scallops also migrate to

The fog rolls in and engulfs the fleet.
(Ralph S. MacKenzie)

103

The culling board is a mixed array of eelgrass and scallops. (*Cape Cod Times* Photo by Milton Moore)

A sea scallop drag (*The Cape Codder*)

avoid the predatory starfish and seek better salinity conditions.

Toward the end of the first day a lot of townspeople drive down to the landing to see how the boats fared. A very distinct protocol governs the first day of the season. Everyone is expected to spread out to look for scallops, but no one is expected to reveal where he caught them. It is a sure sign of a neophyte to talk too rashly about one's catch.

The most severe opprobrium is reserved for those who do not respect their mutual obligation to look for the elusive mollusks. When asked if anyone really did well, one fisherman replies, "Oh yeah, one guy got five bushels; 'course he didn't spread out like the rest of us, jist sat there on the first bed we found." One hopes that the fisherman will enjoy his scallops for he will be remembered for the entire year, until someone else commits a worse faux pas.

It doesn't look like there will be a bonanza this year. A few fishermen will be able to make a decent living, and everyone will have a few quarts of scallop eyes to freeze for the lean winter months. Four years ago, a scallop bonanza did occur. Two fishermen were able to keep the location of scallops a secret for a week. However, when a boat comes in day after day with ten or twelve bushels people start to take notice. Soon there were eleven boats, then twenty. Finally over eighty boats were concentrated over a few acres of bottom. Over a quarter of a million dollars' worth of scallops were extracted from the spot in two weeks. A rush of activity spread through the town as shucking shacks were set up. Sales clerks, insurance salesmen, and carpenters hauled old rusty scallop dredges out of garages and attics where they had languished through former lean years. The sole craftsman who made the dredges was deluged with orders. While the supply lasted the Cape Cod equivalent of a gold rush gripped the towns. The welcome economic boom spread rapidly through the local economy. Sick leave and absenteeism slowed the wheels of regular commerce, but such things are still understood and tolerated on the Cape during scalloping season.

15. Autumnal Migrations

Yet it is not the death sign that the curlews bring but only the memory of life, of a high beauty passing swiftly as the curlew passes, leaving us on an empty beach, with summer gone and a wind blowing.

PETER MATHIESSEN, *The Shorebirds of North America*

It is still dark when the first shots ring out. They echo around the bay and reverberate off the islands. Sea gulls squawk, crows fly, and ducks perish.

It is October 10, the opening day of the "gunning" season. Wet snow swirls around the bay. It is the first time in this century that snow has fallen so early in autumn. The early morning stalwarts, stooped and shivering in the marsh behind the islands, are probably the only people on the East Coast who are happy about the weather.

The hunters' day starts hours before sunrise. They have to feel their way down the bay in darkness in order to be ready for the first flights. The swirling snowflakes sting their eyes and muffles the creak of their oars. With frozen hands they hurry to bail blinds and set decoys before the first gray of dawn pales the eastern sky.

Daylight waxes and with it comes the thunder of distant guns. Geese burst from a faraway marsh and fly out into the early morning sky. They wheel in flight and speed down the channel through a bristling gauntlet of outstretched guns. They have seen the decoys. Will they sweep in toward the waiting blind? Hunters' mouths go dry with anticipation. "Wait! Wait! Wait! They are going to land."

Gliding and zigzagging into the wind, the geese tumble down with extended paddles. As the first goose hits the water the hunters rise and let drive with their powerful shotguns. Two birds fall. One floats, paddles up, in the quiet water in front of the blind. The other goose dives. He has a broken wing. He may escape further hunters, but he will be unable to continue

Geese over the marsh
(Ralph S. MacKenzie)

107

the migration. Slowly he will starve or freeze, to become carrion for scavenging sea gulls.

The days of unbridled hunting are over. From the end of the Civil War until the passage of the Migratory Bird treaty in 1918, market hunting caused untold damage and the extinction of several species.

The slaughter that shore birds suffered was devastating. Some, like the Eskimo curlew, no longer darken the skies with their multitudes. They became known as dough birds because rich deposits of fat would often burst through their breasts when they landed on the hard surface of the marsh. Dunlins were called "simpletons" because of their habit of circling back over the guns to try to rouse their fallen mates. The buff-breasted sandpiper was woefully ignorant of the hunters' deceptions. After their flocks were slaughtered single birds would circle back and call out plaintively to the hunters' decoys. Perhaps the sandpipers preferred the decoys' wooden company to the reality that they were suddenly alone in the world.

Much of the market hunting and poaching was done at night. The hunters would wait for a northeast wind to bring the geese

A sanderling rushing out of the backwash (Ralph S. MacKenzie)

in off the ocean flyway. They would separate between the islands and the marsh so the geese would be forced to fly down a slot between them. The trick was to call the gander. He would lead the flock down through the slot. If one of the hunters killed the gander the rest of the flock would keep circling back to the massacre.

Bird calling was one of the arts of the grim occupation. Calling is actually a form of interspecific sexual communication. Fred Higgins, a colorful guide and sometime-poacher, once put it more graphically: "There is lots of them geese out there and a lot of 'em is horny. You got to sound like the horniest goose on the marsh."

Callers try to mimic three distinct calls. The "hail" or the "pull call" is the call of a lonesome hen. The "feeding call" is a contented clucking noise. If these fail, the hunters try the "come back call."

Before he lost his arm one of Fred Higgins's most effective feeding calls was made by rubbing two quahog shells together. If this didn't work he would put his hat on the edge of the blind and flap his hands on either side of it. The grinding of the quahog shells sounded like feeding ducks and his flapping hands looked like the wings of a male duck rising up to defend his territory.

With today's regulations, hunting does not endanger duck and geese populations. Perhaps it even creates a beneficial closeness, the closeness that occurs in nature between the hunted and the hunter. Indians recognized this closeness when they honored their prey.

No, hunting is not the danger. Hunting gets one close to the marsh. The closer one gets to nature the harder it is to destroy it. Distance does the real damage. More people should get out on a bay, to hear the wild calls of skeins of geese on their lofty passage over the hummocks of the great marsh. They should watch a great blue heron flying against the clouds, its wings beating with the slow and solemn majesty of its ancient heritage. They should feel the chill of recognition that those huge wings and serpentine necks would not have been out of place on the flying reptiles of a far younger world. People who have experienced these things will think twice before allowing a marsh to be drained, filled, and destroyed.

The arrival of the ducks and geese only signaled the peak of the migration. All summer the bay had hosted thousands of less noticeable migrants. The tremulous, liquid calls of whimbrels had sounded over the marsh, and the brilliant white chevrons of willets had flashed in the skies.

Oystercatchers had graced us with their group courtships. The handsome black-and-white birds with brilliant red eyes are renowned for their communal courtship displays. Their name derives from their ability to sneak up on oysters and mussels. They can plunge their bills into the open shells before the mollusk has a chance to snap shut. If the bird is too slow to cut the oyster's abductor muscle the bivalve will clamp down. The incoming tide will drown the hapless bird.

Occasionally I see the phalaropes standing on the shore. Normally they remain far out at sea, where they follow whales in order to feed on their parasites. The females are always larger and more colorful than the males. As we would expect, they are also the aggressors. They compete to mate with the males and then leave them to care for the nestlings.

Ruddy turnstones root along the wrack lines like colorful feathered pigs. These birds receive their name from their habit of turning over stones. The purpose of the behavior was investigated by Mark Gatesby in 1750. A ruddy turnstone was provided with several stones but no food. The bird spent weeks vainly turning over the stones. When the unfortunate bird finally died the scientist concluded that it had starved to death. Science was rather crude in those days.

Every week, killdeer, plovers, and a confusing array of sandpipers or "peeps" arrive from the Arctic tundra. It seems as though the same birds remain throughout the month. Actually they are constantly being replaced by waves of newcomers. Individual birds seldom tarry for long. They pause for a few days to feed in the marsh and probe at the edge of the curling waves. By night they are off on another hundred-mile leg of their 3000-mile journey.

Greater and lesser yellowlegs arrive in September. They run drunkenly through the shallows, weaving from side to side in pursuit of crustacea and minnows. Their crystal-clear calls are a sure harbinger of the rapidly advancing autumn. Dunlins are about the last shore bird to pass through. They race along the beach, probing the sand with their stout bills. The comical bills always look as though they should be on a far larger bird.

Early in September the islands and marsh meadows are covered with flocks of twittering land birds. Warblers, sparrows, and thrushes fly from Spartina head to bayberry bush in their quest for food. Starlings light on the great English locust that somehow rooted on the back of Sampson Island. No one is sure how it got there. The starlings, originally imported from England by a group that wanted to import every bird that appears in Shakespeare's plays, seem to appreciate the tree's Old World

RIGHT Autumn migrations
(Ralph S. MacKenzie)

110

A great blue heron against the clouds
(Howard Solomon)

flavor. They fly through its few remaining leaves and squabble on its gnarled branches.

Hawks have been migrating effortlessly through the highest heavens. I often see them spiraling skyward in the warm updrafts below billowing white cumulus clouds. At the apex of their climb they emerge into the clear blue autumn sky and soar southward toward the next towering cloud.

Sea ducks arrive in late autumn. Flying just above the waves, they appear and disappear against the horizon of the ocean. Soon great rafts of them will bob among the whitecaps of the winter bay.

16. Night Lights of Autumn

The sea from its extreme luminousness presented a wonderful and most beautiful appearance. Every part of the water, which by day is seen as foam, glowed with a pale light. The vessel drove before her bows two billows of liquid phosphorus, and in her wake was a milky train.

CHARLES DARWIN, *Diary of the Voyage of the Beagle*

On a moonless night in November, I sit in the solitude of the empty bay. My fragile skiff appears to float in the center of a hollow sphere of stars. The infinite depths of the autumn sky are reflected star by star on the mirrorlike surface below the boat. The mightly arc of the Milky Way bridges the horizons above and below.

The diminutive flashes of a high-flying jet are lost in the austerity of the night. Noiselessly tracking through the brilliant stars, it appears to be an alien craft in the silent depths of space. Only when it is directly overhead can I hear the plane's familiar roar. It breaks the atmosphere, a crude reminder of man's pervasive domination of the planet. Sailors have told me that even in the solitude of the mid-ocean they are able to navigate to their destinations by following the contrails of jets.

The diminuendo roar ceases, to be replaced by the piping of invisible birds. Migrating across the starry vault, they call to each other to maintain their flock. Out here it does not seem so incredible that they can navigate by the stars. They — as well as I — are suspended in a vast sphere of revolving constellations. They watch as the stars roll out of the eastern ocean and settle in the west. They watch the reflection of the constellations as they wheel majestically overhead. Only the North Star remains motionless at the apex of the axis of the sphere. The birds have only to set their course a few degrees to the side of the unmoving star to accurately align their flight.

Birds have been conducting their migrations at least since the end of the ice age 10,000 years ago. It is difficult to imagine the complex sensory world that they enjoy. They can respond to ultraviolet light, polarized light, and the earth's magnetic field. They can use the sun and the stars in ways we are just discovering, to help them navigate on their fantastic voyages.

The lesser yellowlegs that probe in the soft mud at the edge of the marsh appear to have all the time in the world. Actually they are gorging themselves on food to fuel their nightly flights. They can average over 320 miles per night.

Yellowlegs banded on Cape Cod on August 28 have been recovered six days later on Martinique, 1930 miles away. The arctic terns that hatched on Monomoy Island in July must fly over 9000 miles across the Atlantic Ocean to spend the winter off South Africa.

These smaller birds — the terns, shore birds, and landbirds — tend to travel by night. Some of them can stay aloft for 30 hours at a time. The daytime migrations of the larger birds — the ducks, geese, and herons — are more conspicuous. Their longer wings and ample bodies seem better suited to the ordeal.

Many birds migrate at great heights where oxygen is diffuse. Plovers have been sighted by radar flying 20,000 feet above Pleasant Bay. Mountain climbers have reported seeing geese flying at 29,500 feet over the Himalayas. The mountain climbers, who were using oxygen tanks, found it an exhausting ordeal just to crawl out of their sleeping bags and put on their boots.

Bird migrations have puzzled scientists for a long time. Why do birds undertake these arduous journeys to the north? Why don't they stay in warm southern climates where food is plentiful?

We can surmise that many species of birds lived in the northern hemisphere before the ice ages. The ice ages must have forced them to fly south to obtain food during the winter. But why do they continue to return to the north to reproduce? Is there some aspect of the northern hemisphere that makes it a better place to raise offspring?

Most birds are daylight feeders. At the equator they encounter twelve hours of sunlight every day throughout the year. During the summer, however, the northern latitudes have many more hours of sunlight. Birds can use these extra hours to gather more food, which will hasten the growth of their offspring.

In Alaska it takes nine days for a pair of robins to raise their offspring from egg to fledgling. In Ohio it would take them thirteen days. This means that they have reduced by a third the time that their flightless nestlings are most vulnerable.

These few extra days are a critical margin. If migration can significantly increase their chances of raising a family, then it is understandable why so many birds have adopted this behavior.

RIGHT The larger birds migrate by daylight. (Ralph S. MacKenzie)

114

A plover feeding on scallops (*Cape Cod Times* Photo by Milton Moore)

As I head toward shore I realize the bay has bloomed with light. Blazing pinpoints dot the bottom, and my footprints give off an eerie glow. Millions of tiny motes of living light swirl around before my eyes.

My oar strikes an invisible creature who flashes a brilliant orb about the size of my fist. The nighttime bay has filled with creatures seemingly intent on filling the waters with light.

Noctiluca, planktonic dinoflagellates, are the animals that careened off my legs like underwater Pleides. A transparent cten-ophore, commonly called a comb jelly, emitted the mysterious flash of light. Unlike true jellyfish, comb jellies glide majestically through the water by rhythmically beating rows of cilia. By day they iridesce a delicate bluish green, by night they flash their orbs of annoyance.

Their appearance is an underwater signal of the passing of the season. Autumn has again released nutrients into the bay, which cause this bloom of plants and animals. It will be but a brief grande finale before the curtain falls for winter.

Boulders project through the ice-locked bay. (Ralph S. MacKenzie)

Winter

There is a new sound on the beach, and a greater sound. Slowly and day by day the surf grows heavier and down the long miles of the beach, at the lonely stations men hear the coming winter in the roar.

HENRY BESTON, *The Outermost House*

Buffleheads dive in the deep channels. (*Cape Cod Times* Photo by Milton Moore)

17. Winter

Winter is the time of leanness. The waters of the estuaries tend to be at their clearest. Sunlight comes farther into the water than it did in summer and the water is full of nutrients from the decay of the summer's produce.

JOHN AND MILDRED TEAL, *Life and Death of the Salt Water Marsh*

The bay has returned to nature. The scallop boats and eel boats have retired for the winter. By day the shore is dominated by gulls and geese; at night, by owls and foxes.

The surface waters have changed from a plankton-rich green to a cold hard blue, playthings for winter's tempests. Nor'easters turn the sky the color of pewter, and the bay seethes with waves. The arctic ducks seem content. Their white backs bob vigorously on the thrashing whitecaps. Some scientists think that this coloring is a form of camouflage that allows them to blend with the white waves of their environment. Buffleheads dive in the deep channels and geese climb out on the shore. They huddle in the lee of the bluffs and search for clams along the beach.

A kingfisher sits on the gnarled arm of a scrubby pine and peers into the shallow waters. A pair of great blue herons leave their huge tracks in the sand beside the creek; the few minnows that appear are sluggish and easy to catch. Their half-frozen bodies are swept in and out with the tides. The sugar content of their blood has increased, acting as a natural antifreeze. Most of them have joined the other animals, the crabs and smaller crustacea, that have burrowed into the mud. The mud will remain a few degrees warmer than the water and will protect them from ice. If they touch ice or are taken out of the water, their blood congeals and they die instantly.

A few winter flounder swim listlessly through the remaining patches of eelgrass. Most of the waving green acres of summer eelgrass have been torn from the bottom by autumn storms.

Their dead fronds lie in slowly rotting mats along the shore and will afford numerous crustacea a precarious insulation against the cold. By the end of winter the mats will have deteriorated, leaving the beach clean for next spring. The pristine veneer of the beach will be littered only with the shells of mollusks who perished during winter's adversity.

Knots of eels too young to undertake the autumn migration lie in the soft mud around the bay's many underwater springs. They are attracted by the fresh water, which remains slightly warmer than the salt water of the bay. The same seal that has returned year after year swims near the rock just behind Viking Point. Occasionally, he lifts his doglike face above the surface, a flounder flapping in his mouth.

Eventually, the day comes when a veil of ice appears along the shore. If a cold spell holds, it will spread across the surface. Gradually the entire bay will be locked under a great white sheet of ice. Yet the tides must still rise and fall beneath winter's new white mantle. Dark boulders project through the surging ice, and docks and piers are twisted into grotesque shapes.

Underneath the ice, life goes on as usual, but at a slower pace. Sunlight cannot penetrate the ice sufficiently to support photosynthesis. Without photosynthesis the plankton are at their ebb, the water at its clearest.

As winter progresses, the ice transforms life's simple problems of existence into a series of crises. Winds and tides conspire to push great slabs of ice across the marsh. They shear off the Spartina grasses, but most of the underground rhizomes will remain undamaged to start next year's growth. When the ice stays on the marsh too long it will deplete the oxygen and anaerobic decay will occur. Faint traces of hydrogen sulfide will envelop the marsh, where the lack of oxygen will send fish gulping to the surface.

Winter takes her final bow in a unexpected blizzard that sweeps up from the south. I decide to drive to Truro to view the storm. It is the constant destruction of Truro's high cliffs, forty miles north of Pleasant Bay, that make the bay possible. Snow, sleet, and rain slash against the windshield. The wipers are useless. Clumps of accumulated ice slither back and forth, obscuring my vision of the road ahead.

The peak of the storm will coincide with the highest tide of the month, ensuring the most destructive combination of forces. The radio is warning people to evacuate low-lying areas. The blizzard of '78 swept many Cape Cod houses out to sea.

I park well back from the seaward edge of the parking lot. Each year storms erode a few more yards of parking space. I

RIGHT Underneath the ice, life proceeds at a slower pace. (William Sargent)

cinch up my parka and draw the hood strings tight. Leaning into the icy wind, I fight my way to the edge of the cliff.

Windswept sand, sleet, and icy crystals of salt spray blast up the cliff, lashing my face and body. Seventy feet below, the North Atlantic is a frothing disarray. The waves crisscross and pile on top of each other, as if eager to hurl themselves against the fragile cliffs. A huge wave throws the full fury of its unbroken crest against the bank. The ground trembles with the impact. Air trapped in the curl of the wave explodes with a loud report. As the wave recedes, I hear the sepulchral grinding of rocks drawn across the ocean floor.

Sand is blasted free of the cliff. The next wave dislodges a huge boulder. Its one-ton bulk is finally released from the matrix of glacial till that held it for over ten thousand years. It cascades down the face of the cliff and is lost in the general turmoil. A landslide threatens to carry away the very ground on which I stand. At least ten feet of the cliff and several tons of sand, gravel, and rocks plummet into the waters, which are already brown with eroded clay and mud. They are slightly stained by this new addition.

I have seen enough. Feeling the need for human contact, I drive back down the Cape toward Pleasant Bay. At the head of the bay is an old Victorian building that used to be the Packet Landing Inn, a way station for the coastal sailing packets that carried passengers and produce from New York to Boston. Now it is a local bar where a welcome fire crackles in a cavernous fireplace. The storm has quickened the pace of life and brought people out to get news. One can imagine the Inn as it was a hundred years ago, when local fishermen rubbed shoulders uneasily with fast-talking urban passengers.

A small group huddles around the fire discussing a dramatic rescue off Provincetown. A fishing boat had iced up and floundered in twenty-foot seas. A Coast Guard cutter located the boat and stood by while six men bound themselves together and leaped into the freezing water. The line parted and two men drifted away into the swirling snow. The Coast Guard was able to relocate them, and finally all six were saved.

We could all imagine ourselves drifting off into the darkness, for everyone in the room had experienced a time when the ocean unexpectedly changed from a generous provider to a life-threatening fury. This palpable daily closeness with the dual nature of the ocean gives life on the Cape a poignancy lost to most inland dwellers.

Wrecks and storms fill the psyches of Cape Codders. Year after year wrecks are recounted in minutest detail. An oral his-

Each year, storms claim a few more yards of parking space. (*Cape Cod Times* Photo by Milton Moore)

Spearing eels through the ice
(Ralph S. MacKenzie)

tory bridges the generations so that it is possible to imagine what it was like when *The Montclair, The Sparrow,* or *The Portland* broke up in a previous century. On the bay we remember when Fred Higgins drowned when he fell through the ice while spearing eels, and when Mon Cochran drove his ninety-year-old mother across the frozen bay in his jeep.

Life is not easy on the Cape in the dead of winter. People are caught in a stagnant economy. Self-sufficiency and barter ease the pressure. Fishermen exchange some of their catch for a cord of wood. Those who have not lost the old skills spear eels through the ice and scratch for quahogs along the shore. When chance storms strand thousands of squid on the beach or blow seed scallops onto the shore, people follow the gulls to share the bounty.

But winter on the Cape is a waiting time. Most people and creatures have migrated to warmer climates. Those who remain stoically await the spring.

By the time I return to the bay the weather has changed again. A new front of cold air has pushed the storm out to sea, leaving the bay bathed in the winter moon's silvery luminescence.

A strange silence pervades the night. The newly fallen snow muffles any noise, so that my footsteps sound as if they belong to someone else. The only sign of other humans is a single light bulb that glows weakly from a house on the far side of the bay. Like the animals beneath the ice, I wait for spring.

18. A Winter Visit to Seal Island

Several special factors influence the reproductive strategies of seals, most notably the fact that they are marine mammals that must breed on land.

MARTIN DALY AND MARGOT WILSON, *Sex, Evolution, and Behavior*

It is four in the morning. We have launched a boat in Town Cove in order to film a small herd of harbor seals (*Phoca vitulina cancolor*) on a new island in Nauset inlet.

Cape Cod seals are being devastated by a mysterious disease. Every day more animals wash up on the shore, weak and exhausted. (By the end of the winter over 400 seals will have died from the pneumonia-like disease caused by a type-A animal influenza.)

The New England harbor seal population had been increasing since the early sixties, when the states started to abolish their seal bounties. Seals are a necessary link in the life cycle of the codworm, a parasite that lowers the value of codfish. The bounty on seals was supposed to eradicate the codworms by short-circuiting their life cycles.

Codfish are a favorite food of harbor seals. When the seal eats the fish they also ingest encysted codworm parasites. The high body temperature of the warm-blooded seals induces the codworms to lay eggs. The eggs pass through the seal's digestive tracts and are broadcast into the oceans with the seal's feces. Snails and crabs eat these eggs and are in turn eaten by codfish, thus completing the life cycle. By reducing the seal population state officials had hoped to reduce the codworm populations. I suppose we can draw two conclusions: one, that seal bounties are a heavy-handed means of controlling codworm parasites, and two, that codfish should not be eaten in raw fish sashimi dinners, since the parasites also survive in the congenial warm environment of human stomachs!

The state bounties were superseded by the 1972 Marine Mam-

mal Act that forbade killing or disturbing seals and other marine mammals. Since then, harbor seals have started to increase and reappear in areas where they have not been for decades. The outbreak of this pneumonia would surely slow down that process.

Seal Island was formed a few years ago when a winter storm broke through the barrier beach. A new inlet was created, which isloated this small portion of the barrier beach. The island was no different from the rest of the barrier beach, only a few hundred yards away, yet the fact of its being an island made it a valuable new environment to many species of opportunistic animals. The terns discovered it the first summer of its existence. Separated from the mainland, it was free of foxes, dogs, raccoons, and other land predators. This factor, plus the abundant supplies of silversides in the inlet only yards from their nests, made it a highly attractive new nesting site.

We want to film the seals at sunrise, while the tide is still low and large chunks of peat are exposed. The seals lie on these to soak up the meager warmth of the sun. Mounting the cameras on tripods, we make our way through the dunes that run the length of the island. Beach voles of the Microtus genus scurry off in all directions. The creation of this tiny island has caused a population explosion. The voles are reproducing at an exponential rate because they are isolated from land predators. Only a few hundred yards away the same barrier beach that is still connected to the mainland has only a few scattered voles.

We arrive at the top of the dunes. Below us three seals rest on the large chunks of peat that are the remnants of the ancient marsh. Other seals are in the water. They glance at us with curious faces as they drift by with the outgoing tide. They seem to be enjoying themselves. They swim upstream against the current, then let the outgoing tide carry them down toward the inlet. Occasionally one will dive and surface with a flounder or clam in its mouth.

Side by side on this island, are two species that represent two extremes of behavior. Life for the vole is "nasty, brutish, and short." They are able to conceive even before they are weaned and continue reproducing throughout their lives. Their strategy is to flood the market with offspring, spending as little time as possible nurturing them.

For seals, on the other hand, "less is better." They usually produce only one pup a year and spend a lot of time nurturing it. Generally one finds that animals that pursue the vole stategy occupy transitory environments; puddles that are likely to dry up, or fields that will become forests. They are the pioneers that

Early morning (*The Cape Codder*)

quickly take advantage of a new situation like the formation of this island.

One would expect to find animals that have adopted the strategy of the seal in more stable environments, such as the ocean. In fact, there are some species of wide-ranging birds that tend to adopt the strategy of the seal in the stable tropics while adopting the strategy of the vole in the less predictable temperate zones. In our own species it has been observed that birth rates decrease in more stable economies where the ability to provide adequate nurture is possible.

Normally, animals whose offspring require a great deal of nurturing are monogamous, because it takes the time and energy of both parents to supply all the required nurturing. This is true of many species of birds and is occasionally true for *Homo sapiens*. We might also expect monogamous behavior in seals, but the fact is that they are incorrigibly polygamous.

Why are seals polygamous? The easy answer to all such questions of animal behavior is that the animal in question is a compromise. Of course every animal represents a compromise

between his anatomy, his behavior, and his prior evolution. No animal has completed its evolution. Perhaps the seals can provide some insights into how this works.

Seals belong to the order of Pinnipeds, a group of animals that have made the evolutionary transition from a terrestrial lifestyle to a marine lifestyle. The transition has left them compromised. They are adept and agile underwater but clumsy and vulnerable on land. If they had totally forsaken the land, as the whales have, this would be adequate; however they have not completed the transition. Like so many other animals, they have to return to their former environment to reproduce. This means that they must seek out safe, isolated islands on which to give birth and on which to copulate to produce next year's litter. This severe compromise is critical. Although they can spread out and live peacefully off the vast resources of the ocean most of their lives, during breeding time the males become highly territorial, jealously quarreling over valuable pieces of island real estate.

In most species of Pinnipeds this period of extreme competition has led to the evolution of large competitive males. During the mating season huge bulls collect harems of females on their breeding islands and have to be ever-vigilant of the younger males who hang offshore, waiting to copulate while the harem master isn't looking. In some species the male forsakes eating during the breeding period in order to ensure the fidelity of his willingly faithless females.

In the afternoon I return to Pleasant Bay. A few large flakes of snow drift quietly out of the leaden sky. Only the deep holes and channels remain open, the darkness of their water in stark contrast to the ice-covered bay.

A flock of cormorants huddle around one of these pools. Some stand on the edge of the ice, wings spread to dry, while others attempt to fish. They are being harried by four immature bald eagles. The eagles wait for the cormorants to surface with a fish; then they snatch it away before the frustrated cormorant has a chance to swallow its prize.

The ice cracks and strains with the ebb and flow of the underlying water. The tide is falling; in its wake it leaves a fragile veil of ice on the brown stubble of the marsh. The sunlight catches sudden glints of silver as the air rushes under the icy lattice to replace the withdrawing water.

A fox trots noiselessly along the wrack line. He pauses to scratch the frozen carcass of an eider duck, half encased in a slab of pack ice. Probably the duck died from ingesting too many lead shotgun pellets.

A harbor seal (*Cape Cod Times* Photo by Milton Moore)

131

The fox moves on, his attention now drawn toward the bay. Not far offshore, a flock of geese sit quietly on the edge of an open pool of water. Their quiet gabbling drifts toward the shore. The gander, standing sentry, occasionally surveys the surroundings. Seeing nothing to alarm him, he gives a reassuring feeding chuckle and tucks his head back into the warm comfort of his wing.

The fox feigns indifference to the geese and continues his haphazard progress along the shore. He pauses at the snowy tunnel of a mouse, but an owl has beaten him to the occupant. All at once he whirls and bolts toward a boulder far out in the bay. His ruse has worked. The geese do not notice him. Now he crouches, ears pricked and body atremble, a short distance from the nearest bird.

The fox springs from behind the boulder. He covers the short distance to the nearest goose before she has a chance to untuck her head. The sudden impact bowls her over, but the fox has miscalculated. He sprawls on the slippery ice with a mouthful of fleshless feathers. With a confusion of frantic wings and clamorous honkings, the rest of the flock leaps from the ice. The female is now alone with her adversary.

The fox seizes the leg of the goose. She beats on his head with her powerful wings. He drags her part way toward shore before letting go. The goose slips. This time the fox is ready. He leaps toward her neck — and the struggle is over.

Winter's necessity has spurred the fox to take the life of an animal it would normally never pursue. Life is destined to survive only through the death of other forms of life. It is part of the ongoing process whereby living matter is recycled and evolved to create ever-newer forms. Without this process life would perish, unable to survive the changes of the universe.

Even now, beneath the mantle of ice, life awaits the reawakening. It lies dormant in the stubble of the marsh and the spores of dinoflagellates. It has started to appear with the release of barnacle larvae and the budding of the pink polyps that filament the creeks.

Soon the bay will once again bloom with life. Myriads of new organisms will flush in and out with the tides. Their genes will carry the accumulated knowledge of over two billion years of evolution. They will encounter a new bay, altered this year as it has been every year for the past ten thousand years. A few organisms — through the subtle forces of evolution — will prove to be slightly more fit to survive in the bay's changing environment. On their genes will ride the continuing experiment of life.

RIGHT The gander stands sentry
(Ralph S. MacKenzie)

132

Sea gulls flock to the bay. (Kent H. Wilcoxson, *The Cape Codder*)

Bibliography

Bibliography

Berrill, N. J. *The Life of the Ocean.* New York: McGraw-Hill, 1966.

Beston, Henry. *The Outermost House.* New York: Holt, Rinehart and Winston, 1928.

Buchsbaum, Ralph. *Animals Without Backbones.* Chicago: University of Chicago Press, 1948.

Burton, Maurice. *The Courtship of Animals.* New York: Frederick A. Praeger Publishers, 1946.

Carson, Rachel. *The Edge of the Sea.* Boston: Houghton Mifflin Company, 1955.

————. *The Sea Around us.* New York: Oxford University Press, 1961.

————. *Under Sea Wind.* New York: The American Library, 1941.

Chamberlain, Barbara Blau. "The Dynamic History of Cape Cod." *Natural History Magazine,* May 1967.

————. *These Fragile Outposts: A Geological Look at Cape Cod, Martha's Vineyard, and Nantucket.* New York: Doubleday and Company, Inc., 1964.

Cole, John N. *Striper: A Story of Fish and Man.* Boston: Little, Brown and Company, 1978.

Cooper, Elizabeth K. *Science on the Shores and Banks.* New York: Harcourt Brace, 1960.

Fiske, John D. *A Study of the Marine Resources of Pleasant Bay.* Department of Natural Resources, Commonwealth of Massachusetts, Monograph Series, no. 5, May 1967.

Gates, David A. *Seasons of the Salt Marsh.* Old Greenwich, Connecticut: Chatham Press, Inc., 1975.

Gosner, Kenneth L. *A Field Guide to the Atlantic Seashore.* Boston: Houghton Mifflin Company, 1979.

Gross, Grant M. *Oceanography.* Columbus, Ohio: Charles E. Merrill Publishing Company, 1967.

Hardy, Alister C. *The Open Sea: Its Natural History.* Boston: Houghton Mifflin Company, 1971.

Hay, John. *Nature's Year*. New York: Ballantine Books, Inc., 1961.

———. *The Run*. New York: Ballantine Books Inc., 1959.

Hough, Henry Beetle. *Soundings at Sea Level*. Boston: Houghton Mifflin Company, 1980.

Ketchum, Bostwick H. *The Water's Edge*. Cambridge: MIT Press, 1972.

Kittredge, Henry C. *Cape Cod: Its People and Their History*. Boston: Houghton Mifflin Company, 1968.

———. *Mooncussers of Cape Cod*. Boston: Houghton Mifflin Company, 1937.

Koper, Phillip. *The Wild Edge*. New York: Times Books, 1979.

Richardson, Wyman. *The House on Nauset Marsh*. Old Greenwich, Connecticut: Chatham Press, Inc., 1972.

Robbins, Sarah F., and Clarice Yeatsch. *The Sea Is All About Us*. Salem, Massachusetts: Peabody Museum Press, 1973.

Roueche, Berton. *What's Left*. Boston: Little, Brown and Company, 1968.

Rudloe, Jack. *The Erotic Ocean*. New York: World Publishing Company, 1971.

Steinbeck, John, and Edward Ricketts. *The Sea of Cortez*. New York: Viking Press, 1941.

Strahler, George N. *A Geologist's View of Cape Cod*. Garden City, New York: Natural History Press. Doubleday and Company, Inc., 1966.

Teal, John, and Mildred Teal. *Life and Death of a Salt Marsh*. Boston: Little, Brown and Company, 1969.

Thoreau, Henry David. *Cape Cod*. Edited by Dudley C. Lunt. New Haven: College and University Press, 1951.

Tinbergen, Niko. *The Animal in Its World*. Cambridge: Harvard University Press, 1972.

———. *The Herring Gull's World*. New York: Harper and Row, 1971.

Warner, William. *Beautiful Swimmers*. Boston: Little, Brown and Company, 1976.

Shallow Waters has been set in VIP Bembo, a film adaptation of the 1929 English Monotype issue, based by Stanley Morison on the first Aldine roman. The original design was cut in 1495 by Francesco Griffo da Bologna for the Venetian publisher and printer Aldus Manutius for his edition of Pietro Bembo's *De Aetna*. Bembo remains an elegant and pure example of old style design.

COMPOSITOR DEKR Corporation
PRINTER The Alpine Press
BINDER The Book Press